TOP 10

ANDALUCIA
& COSTA DEL SOL

JEFFREY KENNEDY

DK

EYEWITNESS TRAVEL

Left **La Mezquita, Córdoba** Right **Ronda**

LONDON, NEW YORK,
MELBOURNE, MUNICH AND DELHI
www.dk.com

Produced by Sargasso Media Ltd, London

Reproduced by Colourscan, Singapore
Printed and bound in China by Leo Paper
Products Ltd

First published in Great Britain in 2004
by Dorling Kindersley Limited
80 Strand, London WC2R 0RL
A Penguin Company

Copyright 2004, 2010
© Dorling Kindersley Limited,
London

Reprinted with revisions 2006, 2008, 2010

A CIP catalogue record is available
from the British Library.

ISBN 978-1-40535-194-2

Within each Top 10 list in this book, no
hierarchy of quality or popularity is implied.
All 10 are, in the editor's opinion, of roughly
equal merit.

We're trying to be cleaner and greener:
• we recycle waste and switch things off
• we use paper from responsibly managed
  forests whenever possible
• we ask our printers to actively reduce
  water and energy consumption
• we check out our suppliers' working
  conditions – they never use child labour

Find out more about our values and
best practices at www.dk.com

Contents

Andalucía's Top 10

The information in this DK Eyewitness Top 10 Travel Guide is checked regularly.
Every effort has been made to ensure that this book is as up-to-date as possible at the time of
going to press. Some details, however, such as telephone numbers, opening hours, prices,
gallery hanging arrangements and travel information are liable to change. The publishers cannot
accept responsibility for any consequences arising from the use of this book, nor for any
material on third party websites, and cannot guarantee that any website address in this book
will be a suitable source of travel information. We value the views and suggestions of our
readers very highly. Please write to: Publisher, DK Eyewitness Travel Guides,
Dorling Kindersley, 80 Strand, London, Great Britain WC2R 0RL.

Cover: Front – **Getty Images**: Digital Vision/ABEL clb; **Photolibrary**: John Arnold Images/Peter Adams main.
Spine – **DK Images**: Neil Lukas b. Back – **DK Images**: Linda Whitwam cra, tl; Peter Wilson ca, cla.

Left **Alcalá La Real** Right **Costa del Sol**

Left **View of La Mezquita, Córdoba** Right **Pueblo blanco, Cádiz Province**

Key to abbreviations
Adm *admission charge* **Free** *no admission charge* **Dis. access** *disabled access*

3

ANDALUCÍA'S TOP 10

TOP 10 Andalucía's Highlights

The diverse and politically semi-autonomous region of Andalucía has a population of some 8 million and embodies what is thought of as typically Spanish – an accurate portrait of the place and its people must include the bullfight, flamenco, gypsies, remote white villages, high sierras and mass tourism on endless stretches of beach. The memories you take with you after a visit here will be colourful, joyous, intense and deeply stirring.

Moorish Granada 1
Andalucía's 1,300-year-old Moorish heritage evokes pure Romanticism that is hard to equal. The delicate art and architecture is among the most splendid to be found on European soil *(see pp8–13)*.

Seville Cathedral and La Giralda 2
These two chief wonders of Seville beautifully embody the juxtaposition of the Moors and the triumphalism of their Christian conquerors *(see pp14–15)*.

Real Alcázar, Seville 3
A mix of styles is evident in this vast and luxurious pleasure palace, built almost entirely by Moorish artisans on behalf of their Christian overlords, including the lush gardens *(see pp16–17)*.

Córdoba City & La Mezquita 4
This was once the most important city in Europe, a fact that is illustrated by the architectural masterpiece of La Mezquita, the Great Mosque *(see pp18–21)*.

Cádiz 5
Said to be Europe's oldest city, Cádiz still retains an aura of age-old mystery. The golden-domed cathedral on the waterfront is a spectacular sight *(see pp22–3)*.

Map labels: Guadiana · Peñarroya-Pueblonuevo · Espiel · CÓRDOBA · Aroche · Jabugo · Aracena · Cazalla de la Sierra · Córdoba 4 · Cabezas Rubias · Minas de Riotinto · Lora del Río · Guadalquivir · Écija · Montilla · HUELVA · Gibraleón · Seville 2 3 · SEVILLA · Estepa · Ayamonte · Huelva · Almonte · Alcalá de Guadaira · Osuna · Punta Umbría · El Rocío · Dos Hermanas · Utrera · Olmera · Atlantic Ocean · Parque Nacional del Coto Doñana 9 · Algodonales · MÁLAGA · Jerez de la Frontera · Arcos de la Frontera · Ronda 6 · Rota · CÁDIZ · Cádiz 5 · Puerto Real · Marbella · San Fernando · Alcalá de los Gazules · Estepona · Costa de la Luz · Vejer de la Frontera · Los Barrios · La Línea de la Concepción · Algeciras · Gibraltar (to U.K)

6 Ronda

The largest of several white villages *(pueblos blancos)* scattered throughout the region, Ronda is built on a table of rock that is spectacularly split by the Tajo gorge. It is also reputed to be the birthplace of the modern style of bull-fighting *(see pp24–5)*.

7 Costa del Sol

From the wealthiest of the yachting-set enclaves to all-inclusive package deals for young families, this famous expanse of sand and former fishing villages has something for everyone *(see pp26–7)*.

8 Baeza & Úbeda

Both of these exquisite towns in Jaén Province offer world-class Renaissance architecture set in perfectly preserved historic centres *(see pp28–9)*.

9 Parque Nacional del Coto Doñana

The vast delta of the Guadalquivir River constitutes one of the world's most important nature reserves, without which birdlife throughout Europe would be seriously compromised. The zone has a fascinating mix of terrains, but can be visited on guided tours only *(see pp30–31)*.

10 Sierra Nevada

Europe's second highest mountain range after the Alps offers the continent's southernmost ski resort, a wealth of wildlife for trekkers to wonder at, and dozens of remote villages along its southern slopes that preserve ancient cultural traditions and unique forms of vernacular architecture *(see pp32–3)*.

Moorish Granada: The Alhambra

The great complex of the Alhambra is the best-preserved medieval Arab palace in the world and, with nearly two million visitors annually, it is also the most popular monument in Spain. Built on the largely inaccessible Sabika Hill overlooking the city of Granada, its most distinctive phase began in the 11th century as the qa'lat al-Hamra (Red Fort) of the Ziridian rulers. From the 13th to almost the end of the 15th century the kings of the succeeding Nasrid dynasty embellished the site in a most spectacular fashion. The later Christian additions, although handsome in their own right, are generally thought to clash with the delicate, evocative architecture of the Moors.

View of the Alhambra

🍴 There are snacks and drinks available within the compound, but taking your own bottle of water is a good idea.

🎫 Visitor numbers are restricted, so avoid queues by booking tickets in advance, through your hotel, by phone (902 44 12 21) or online at www.alhambra-patronato.es

It is possible to rent an audio-guide that explains the history and use of each area within the complex.

- Map S2
- Open Mar–Oct: 8:30am–8pm daily, 10–11:30pm Tue–Sat; Nov–Feb: 8:30am–6pm daily, 8–9:30pm Fri–Sat; Closed 1 Jan, 25 Dec
- Adm €12.00
- Museo de la Alhambra: Open 9am–2:30pm Tue–Sat
- Free

Top 10 Features

1. Puerta de la Justicia
2. Puerta del Vino
3. Plaza de los Aljibes
4. Alcazaba
5. Palacio de Carlos V
6. Palacios Nazaríes
7. Palacio de Mexuar
8. Palacio de Comares
9. Palacio de los Leones
10. Partal

Puerta de la Justicia
Built in 1348, this magnificent horseshoe arch *(above)* makes use of Arab defensive techniques – a steep approach combined with four right-angled turns – to slow down invading armies.

Puerta del Vino
The "Wine Gate" – so called because it was used as a wine cellar in the 16th century – marks the main entrance arch to what was once the Medina (market).

Plaza de los Aljibes
From these ramparts *(below)* visitors can enjoy superb views of Granada. The giant cisterns *(aljibes)* underneath were built by the Christian conquerors.

Alcazaba
Although largely in ruins, this fortress is well worth a look. Don't miss climbing up onto the Torre de la Vela for views of the Sierra Nevada.

Each ticket is marked with a half-hour time slot of entrance into the Nasrid Palaces, which cannot be changed.

5 Palacio de Carlos V

This Italian Renaissance palace is the masterpiece of Pedro Machuca, a student of Michelangelo. Housed here are the Museo de la Alhambra, with a fine collection of Nasrid art, and the Museo de Bellas Artes, with a range of interesting Christian works.

Plan of the Alhambra

Generalife

Main entrance

6 Palacios Nazaríes

The Nasrid palaces are built of simple brick, wood and stucco, in keeping with Islamic thought not to compete with the creations of Allah.

9 Palacio de los Leones

Dating from the late 1300s, this palace *(below)* was the Harem, the private zone reserved for the sultan and his family. The fountain of 12 lions, currently under restoration, may represent the 12 signs of the zodiac, 12 hours of the clock, or the 12 tribes of Israel.

7 Palacio de Mexuar

The most poorly preserved of the three palaces, this area *(below)* was the most public space, dedicated to judicial and bureaucratic business. The original structure dates from 1365, but there are obvious Christian overlays, since it was converted to a chapel in the 16th century.

8 Palacio de Comares

Built in the mid-14th century, this area constituted the *Serallo*, where the sultan would receive dignitaries and deal with diplomatic issues. Inside is the Salón de Embajadores, the main throne room of the Alhambra. In front of the palace is the Patio de Arrayanes *(above)*, where serene fountains and pools, fragrant plantings, and elaborate wood and stucco work are all strictly geometric in design yet delicately refined, often featuring inscribed poems in praise of Allah.

10 Partal

As you leave the Alhambra, stroll through the gardens and watercourses laid out in an area that used to have palaces of its own. All you can see of them now are five porticoed arches *(below)*. This area leads up to the Generalife, the summer palace. *(see pp10–11)*.

Buses 32 and 34 travel between the Alhambra and the Albaicín. The journey takes 10–15 minutes.

9

Left **Jardines Altos** Right **Teatro**

Moorish Granada: Generalife

The Towers

Following the gardens of the Partal *(see p9)* as you walk towards the Generalife, you will encounter a number of restored Moorish towers built into the wall. The Torre de los Picos, Torre del Cadí, Torre de la Cautiva, Torre de las Infantas, Torre del Cabo de la Carrera and Torre del Agua are all worth a look for their fine detail, as well as for the views they command. The Torre de la Cautiva and the Torre de las Infantas are twin tower-palaces with richly decorated rooms.

Plan of Generalife

The Hill of the Sun

A footbridge flanked by two towers takes you over to the hill that rises above the Alhambra. A vast summer palace once stood here, amid 75 acres of gardens, which predated the Alhambra by a century, although little of it now remains.

The Name of the Garden

The word Generalife is generally considered to be a corruption of the Arab phrase *Djinat al-Arif*, which can be translated as "the Architect's Garden" (referring to Allah) or simply "the Best Garden" or "the High Garden". In an impressive engineering feat the Darro River was diverted 18 km (11 miles) to provide water for this lush sanctuary.

Teatro

The first thing you will encounter as you climb the hill is the amphitheatre, nestled into a tree-lined hollow. Dance performances and musical concerts are offered here as part of an annual festival of the arts.

Jardines Nuevos

The "New Gardens" are also called the Lower Gardens, and it is clear at a glance that they owe little to Moorish taste. Hedges and formal patterns echo the

Torre de los Picos

The Generalife is included in the ticket to the Alhambra, but is not open late night hours.

Jardines Nuevos

Italian style, but the sound of running water creates a soothing atmosphere in keeping with the Moorish ideal. In Islam, Paradise is defined as an oasis – a water garden full of fragrant blossoms.

Jardines Altos

As you reach the entrance to the upper gardens, you will first encounter the Patio de Polo, where visitors would leave their horses before ascending to the palace. On this level you will be welcomed by a series of fountains and formal plantings, interlaced with walkways and copses.

Patio de la Acequia

The "Court of the Long Pool" is the most famous water spectacle of the garden. Perfectly proportioned pools are set off by rows of water jets. At one end stands one of the complex's most harmonious buildings, the Sala Regia, with its decorated arcades and airy portico.

Patio de los Cipreses

The Court of the Cypresses is also known as the Patio de la Sultana, for this is where Zoraya, the wife of Boabdil *(see p35)*, is said to have secretly met her lover, the chief of the Abencerrajes clan. The sultan had the chief's men massacred upon discovery of the infidelity. A 700-year-old cypress tree commemorates the trysting place.

Escalera del Agua

These staircases above the palace, also known as the Camino de las Cascadas, have handrails that double as watercourses. They are best in spring, when the wisteria is in bloom.

Leaving the Gardens

As you exit the gardens you will pass along the Paseo de las Adelfas and the Paseo de los Cipreses, lined respectively with oleanders and cypresses. Back to the Hill of the Sun, take Cuesta del Rey Chico down to the Albaicín *(see pp12–13)*.

History of the Alhambra

This picturesque castle was the last bastion of al-Andalus, the Moorish hegemony that, at its height, included almost the entire Iberian Peninsula. By 1237 the Christians had reconquered all but this emirate, but the Moors managed to flourish here for some 250 years longer, only succumbing to the forces of King Fernando and Queen Isabel in 1492 *(see p34)*. The Generalife was the summer palace to which the Moorish leaders could escape the political life of the palace and the bustling city below and relax in the beautifully landscaped grounds. After centuries of neglect, and attempts by Napoleon's army to blow the palace up, the Moorish structures were preserved in the early 19th century, after the American writer Washington Irving inspired the world with his popular travel journal entitled *Tales of the Alhambra (see p57)*.

Left **Real Chancillería** Right **El Bañuelo**

🔟 Moorish Granada: Albaicín

1 Real Chancillería
The austerely impressive Royal Chancery dates from 1530, built shortly after the *reconquista* as part of the futile attempt to Christianize this Moorish quarter. The palace is attributed to architect Diego de Siloé. ✆ *Map Q2*

2 Iglesia de Santa Ana
At the end of Plaza Nueva stands this 16th-century brick church in Mudéjar style, built by Muslim artisans for Christian patrons. Inside the main chapel is a coffered ceiling in the Moorish tradition. The belltower was originally a minaret. ✆ *Map R2*

3 El Bañuelo (Baños Arabes)
Dating from the 11th century, these are the best preserved Moorish baths in Spain. They comprise several rooms that were used for changing, meeting, massage and bathing. ✆ *Carrera del Darro 31 • 958 02 78 00 • Map R2 • Open 10am–2pm Tue–Sat • Free*

4 Casa de Castril
This ornate 16th-century mansion was originally owned by the secretary to King Fernando and Queen Isabel. Since 1879 it has served as the Archaeological and Ethnological Museum, displaying artifacts from Granada's past, from the Paleolithic era up until the

Map of Albaicín

Reconquest in 1492. A highlight is the 14th-century astrolabe, by which Moorish scientists could track the movements of the stars. ✆ *Carrera del Darro 43 • Map R2 • Open 2:30–8:30pm Tue, 9am–8:30pm Wed–Sat & 9am–2:30pm Sun • Adm (free for EU members)*

5 Iglesia de San Pedro y San Pablo
Across the road from the Casa de Castril, this church also dates from the 1500s and graces an attractive spot on the banks of the river. From here you can see the towers of the Alhambra dominating the landscape. ✆ *Map R2*

6 Paseo de los Tristes
This tree-lined esplanade follows the course of the river upstream. It is broad enough to have once accommodated tournaments and processions, but now restaurants and bars dominate the scene. ✆ *Map S2*

Casa de Castril

The Albaicín, Granada's Moorish quarter, is situated on the hill facing the Alhambra. The area is a popular spot for pickpockets.

View from El Mirador de San Nicolás

Plaza Larga
From the Paseo de los Tristes follow Calle Panaderos to reach this busy market square, where you'll find mostly produce stalls as well as cheap eateries and bars. The square sports an Islamic gateway with a typically angled entrance as part of what remains of the upper fortifications. This is the Arco de las Pesas – if you pass through it you will come to the Albaicín's most popular square, Plaza San Nicolás. ⊗ *Map R1*

El Mirador de San Nicolás
This magnificent terrace in front of the Iglesia de San Nicolás has such lovely views of the Alhambra and the Sierra Nevada that it has long been dubbed El Mirador ("The Lookout Point") de San Nicolás. The views are extraordinary at sunset, when the Alhambra glows softly ochre and the often snow-capped Sierra Nevada radiates pink in the distance. ⊗ *Map R1*

Tearooms
As you wander around the labyrinth of whitewashed houses and tiny sloping alleyways of the Albaicín quarter you will encounter many tearooms – a Moroccan tradition that is very much alive in this quarter. Possibly the best one, La Tetería del Bañuelo *(see p116)*,

consists of a series of rooms set amid delightful gardens. Here you can sip your minty brew, nibble honeyed sweets and contemplate the timeless panorama.

Moroccan Shops
Check out the hilly streets off Calle Elvira, especially Caldería Vieja and Caldería Nueva, for typically Moroccan shops. The scene is indistinguishable from what you would find in Morocco itself, with the colourful wares spilling out onto the pavements *(see p114)*.

Sacromonte Gypsy Caves

Leaving the Albaicín quarter to the north, follow the Camino del Sacromonte to reach the hill of the same name. The so-called "Holy Hill" is most noted for the presence of some 3,500 caves traditionally inhabited by gypsies (see p59). For more than six centuries, the zone has been notorious for wild goings-on, most especially *zambras*, impromptu gypsy fiestas of flamenco music and dance, and outsiders have always been welcome to witness their cultural celebrations. Today some 80 percent of the caves are still occupied and several of them continue to operate as venues for tourist spectacles.

Sacromonte

For information on flamenco events call Centro de Interpretación del Sacromonte (958 21 51 20, www.sacromontegranada.com)

▓10 Seville Cathedral & La Giralda

In 1248, after some 500 years of Islamic culture, Seville was reconquered by Christian forces, who paradoxically threatened the Moorish inhabitants with full-scale massacre if they damaged any of the city's magnificent edifices. Pragmatically, the conquerors simply rededicated the huge Almohad mosque to the Virgin and for about 150 years used it as their principal place of worship. In 1401, however, the momentous decision was taken to demolish the then mouldering building and erect a new cathedral of unprecedented proportions on its enormous rectangular base. In just over a century, the structure was complete, the renowned minaret now serving as the belltower.

Main entrance

🔴 **For fabulous views of the cathedral and the Giralda, visit the elegant rooftop bar at EME fusionhotel (see p138).**

🟢 **The climb up La Giralda is fairly easygoing thanks to the 35 broad ramps, designed to accommodate a man on horseback. The view makes it well worth the ascent.**

- *Plaza Virgen de los Reyes*
- *Map M4*
- *954 21 49 71*
- *www.catedralde sevilla.es*
- *Open 11am–5:30pm Mon–Sat, 2:30–6:30pm Sun (Jul & Aug: 9:30am–4:30pm)*
- *Services 8:30am, 9am, 10am, noon, 5pm Mon–Sat; 8:30am, 11am, noon, 1pm, 5pm, 6pm Sun*
- *Adm €8.00*

Top 10 Features

1. Exterior and Scale
2. Puerta del Perdón
3. Patio de los Naranjos
4. Museo de Obras y Pintura Sevillana
5. Interior
6. Capilla Mayor
7. Sacristía de los Cálices
8. Sacristía Mayor
9. Sala Capitular
10. La Giralda

1 Exterior and Scale

In sheer cubic vastness, Seville Cathedral *(right)* is the largest Christian church in the world, and there's a certificate from the Guinness Book of Records on display here to prove it. It measures 126 m (415 ft) by 83 m (270 ft) and the nave rises to 43 m (140 ft). The best place to take it all in is from La Giralda.

2 Puerta del Perdón

The "Gate of Pardon" is set in a crenellated wall and is the main entrance to the only surviving section of the mosque. The arch and bronze-covered doors are a masterpiece of Almohad art, carved with 880 Koranic inscriptions. There are also sculpted Renaissance elements, most notably a bas-relief depicting the Expulsion of the Moneychangers from the Temple.

3 Patio de los Naranjos

The Courtyard of Orange Trees *(below)* was the place where ritual ablutions were performed before entering the mosque for prayer.

For more places of worship See pp40–41

Museo de Obras y Pintura Sevillana

Located to the left of the main cathedral entrance, this museum displays 12 paintings and several sculptures from the 17th-century Sevillian School, which included artists such as Bartolomé Esteban Murillo, Francisco de Zurbarán and Francisco Pacheco.

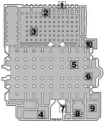

Capilla Mayor

The main altar's *tour de force* is its 15th-century *retablo*, which is the world's largest altarpiece *(above)*. Composed of gilded carved wood, it boasts some 45 Biblical scenes employing some 1,000 figures.

Sacristía de los Cálices

Part of the cathedral's treasury is housed here. The anteroom displays the Tenebrario, a 7.8 m (25-ft) Plateresque candelabrum used during Holy Week. Inside, the star turns are a painting by Goya of Seville's patron saints, Justa and Rufina *(above)*, as well as canvases by Zurbarán, Jordaens and other Masters.

Sacristía Mayor

The Main Sacristy is dominated by a dome *(left)*, designed in the 16th century. The centrepiece of the sacristy is a 450-kg (990-lb), 3-m (10-ft) silver Baroque monstrance created by Juan de Arfe.

Plan of the Cathedral

Sala Capitular

The Chapter House contains Murillo's *Immaculate Conception* in the vault and boasts a lavish marble floor.

La Giralda

This grand tower *(above)* is the symbol of Seville, built between 1172 and 1195. It takes its name from the weathervane on top, called *El Giraldillo*.

Semana Santa Festivities

Seville's Holy Week celebrations leading up to Easter *(see p60)* are Andalucía's richest and most renowned. Here, 57 brotherhoods *(cofradías)* compete to bear aloft the most well-dressed Virgin in mourning and an image from the Passion of Christ. Floats are carried by *costaleros* (bearers), while the processions are lead by *nazarenos* – penitents donning conical hoods.

Interior

Inside the cathedral the Gothic arches are so high that the building is said to have its own independent climate.

Real Alcázar, Seville

This extensive complex embodies a series of palatial rooms and spaces in various styles and from various ages. The front towers and walls constitute the oldest surviving section, dating from AD 913 and built by the Emir of Córdoba, Abd el-Rahman III, most likely on the ruins of Roman barracks. A succession of caliphs added their dazzling architectural statements over the ensuing centuries. Then came the Christian kings, particularly Pedro I the Cruel (or the Just) in the 14th century, and finally the rather perfunctory 16th-century apartments of Carlos V. Much of the structure underwent major modifications as recently as the 18th century, due to earthquake damage.

View of the Real Alcázar

🛈 The Alcázar has a flow-control entry system whereby limited numbers of people are allowed in every half hour. To avoid long waits, visit at off-peak times.

- *Patio de Banderas*
- *Map M4*
- *954 50 23 24*
- *www.patronato-alcazarsevilla.es*
- *Open Apr–Sep: 9:30am–7pm Tue–Sun, Oct–Mar: 9:30am–5pm Tue–Sun*
- *Closed 1 & 6 Jan, Good Friday, 25 Dec*
- *Adm €7.50*

Top 10 Features

1. Puerta del León
2. Sala de Justicia
3. Patio del Yeso
4. Patio de la Montería
5. Casa de la Contratación
6. Patio de las Doncellas
7. Salón de Embajadores
8. Patio de las Muñecas
9. Palacio Gótico
10. Gardens

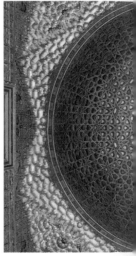

Puerta del León
The entrance gate into the first courtyard *(above)* is flanked by original Almohad walls. Note the Gothic and Arabic inscriptions on the interior façade.

Sala de Justicia
Here and in adjacent halls and courts is some of the purest Mudéjar art to be found, commissioned by Alfonso XI of Castile around 1330 and executed by craftsmen from Granada. The star-shaped coffered ceiling and fine plasterwork are quite exquisite.

Patio del Yeso
The secluded Court of Plaster, greatly restored, is one of the few remnants of the 12th-century palace. The delicate stucco work features scalloped arches *(below)* and is set off by a shady garden with water channels.

For more alcázars in Andalucía See pp38–9

4 Patio de la Montería

The Hunting Courtyard has 14th-century Mudéjar decorative work – a perfect synthesis of differing cultural influences.

5 Casa de la Contratación

These halls are where Fernando and Isabel met with the explorers of the New World.

7 Salón de Embajadores

The most brilliant room in the entire Alcázar. Its crowning glory is the dazzling dome of carved, painted and gilded wood *(below)*, inscribed in Arabic as having been constructed by craftsmen from Toledo and completed in 1366.

Plan of the Real Alcázar

9 Palacio Gótico

In a refurbished 13th-century Gothic structure built by Alfonso X the Wise, this palace *(above)* has a rather inharmonious Renaissance styling.

10 Gardens

Moorish touches – fountains, pools, orange groves, palms and hedgerows – abound in these gardens. Concerts and events are held here on summer evenings.

6 Patio de las Doncellas

The Court of the Maidens *(above)* commemorates the annual tribute of 100 virgins delivered to the Moorish rulers by the Christians. The *azulejos* (tiles) are fine examples of Granada craftsmanship.

8 Patio de las Muñecas

The intimate Court of the Dolls *(below)* was the living room of the palace and is named after two faces carved into the base of one of the arches.

Pedro I

Few Spanish kings have received such contradictory press over the centuries as Pedro I (1350–69). Called both "the Cruel" and "the Just", he killed his own brother in order to consolidate his position and flaunted his cohabitation with his mistress María de Padilla. The alcázar we see today is almost entirely the result of Pedro's rebuilding programme, primarily so that he and María would have a cosy place of retreat.

> Mudéjar architecture is a blend of Moorish building styles and Christian themes and imagery.

🔟 Córdoba City

The main sight in Córdoba City is undoubtedly the Great Mosque, La Mezquita – one of the unsurpassed masterpieces of world architecture. But the entire city, in all its immaculately whitewashed splendour, is a major jewel in Andalucía's crown. In addition to the mosque and its incongruous but splendid cathedral within, other sights here include fine monuments and palaces from every age, art and history museums, one of Andalucía's greatest archaeological repositories, and a rather gruesome yet fascinating museum dedicated to the glories of the bullfight.

Palacio de los Marqueses de Viana

⏵ **Head for the Puente Romano at sunset for glowing views.**

- Map D3
- Alcázar: Campo Santo de los Mártires; 957 42 01 51; Open 8:30am–7:30pm Tue–Fri, 9:30am–4:30pm Sat, 9:30am–2:30pm Sun; Adm €4.00
- Baños del Alcázar Califal: Campo Santo de los Mártires; Open as the Alcázar; Adm €2.00 (free Wed)
- Museo de Bellas Artes: Plaza del Potro 1; 957 35 55 50; Open 2:30–8:30pm Tue, 9am–8:30pm Wed–Sat, 9am–2:30pm Sun; Adm €1.50
- Museo Arqueológico: Plaza Jerónimo Páez 7; 957 35 55 17; Open 9am–8:30pm Tue–Sat (from 2:30pm Tue); Adm €1.50
- Palacio de los Marqueses de Viana: Plaza Don Gome 2; 957 49 67 41; Open 10am–7pm Tue–Sat, 10am–3pm Sun; Adm €6.00
- Museo Torre de la Calahorra: Puente Romano; 957 29 39 29; Open 10am–6pm daily (summer: 10am–2pm & 4:30–8:30pm); Free

Top 10 Sights
1. La Mezquita
2. Judería
3. Alcázar de los Reyes Cristianos
4. Baños del Alcázar Califal
5. Museo de Bellas Artes
6. Plaza del Potro
7. Museo Arqueológico
8. Palacio de los Marqueses de Viana
9. Museo Torre de la Calahorra
10. Puente Romano

1 La Mezquita
The world's third-largest mosque *(below)* remains a place of grandeur and mystical power *(see pp20–21).*

2 Judería
All around the Mezquita is the city's ancient Jewish quarter, dating back to the time of the Roman Empire. Its narrow alleyways are brilliantly whitewashed, hung with flowerpots, and graced with beautiful Moorish patios. This district also has Andalucía's only medieval synagogue, built in 1315.

3 Alcázar de los Reyes Cristianos
This fortified palace, built in 1328, was used by the Inquisition (1500s–1820) and as a prison (until the 1950s). But today it is tranquil, with gardens, water terraces and fountains *(above).*

4 Baños del Alcázar Califal
Built in the 10th century, these Arab baths *(above)* reflect the classical order of Roman baths, with cold, warm and hot rooms.

5 Museo de Bellas Artes

A former 16th-century charity hospital is now the city's main art museum. It has a collection of works by local painters and sculptors, as well as paintings and drawings by Masters such as Goya, Ribera, Murillo, Zurbarán, and Valdés Leal.

8 Palacio de los Marqueses de Viana

This noble residence (14th- to 18th-century) includes preserved period rooms and furnishings *(above)*.

Map of Córdoba

10 Puente Romano

Crossing the Río Guadalquivir, this massive arched bridge *(above)* has Roman foundations, although it was rebuilt by the Moors. Halfway across is a statue of the Archangel Raphael, whom the people of the city still honour with flowers for saving it from the plague.

6 Plaza del Potro

This small but elegant square, adorned with a 16th-century fountain *(above)*, was once the livestock market.

7 Museo Arqueológico

Housed in a Renaissance mansion, this is one of the region's best archaeological museums. A highlight is the 10th-century Moorish bronze of a stag, found at Medina Azahara *(see p119)*.

9 Museo Torre de la Calahorra

Part of a Moorish castle that controlled access to the city, the tower *(below)* is now home to the Roger Garaudy Three Cultures Museum, which explains how Muslims, Christians and Jews lived side by side in medieval Córdoba. There are impressive views of the city from the tower battlements.

Multicultural Tradition

Córdoba's brilliance owes much to its rich multicultural history. Its most important edifices are emblematic of the cross-fertilization of Islamic, Christian and Jewish cultures, and at its height in the 10th century, Córdoba was the spiritual and scientific centre of the Western World, due to its policy of religious tolerance *(see p34)*. However, following the Christian *reconquista*, many non-Christian thinkers were banished and the city soon fell into decline.

10 La Mezquita, Córdoba

Although it has officially been a Christian site for almost nine centuries, La Mezquita's identity as a mosque is inescapable – notwithstanding the cathedral insensitively placed in its centre like a huge spider in its web. As with the Alhambra (see pp8–9), Emperor Carlos V can be blamed for this aesthetic indiscretion. Overriding the wishes of Córdoba's mayor, Carlos authorized the cathedral's construction in the 16th century, although he deeply regretted his decision upon beholding the completed travesty. Yet, despite time's every indignity, the world's third-largest mosque remains a place of grandeur, glory and ineffable mystical power.

View of La Mezquita

🍴 **El Caballo Rojo** *(C/Cardenal Herrero 28 • 957 47 53 75 • €€€)* is located just across from the Puerta del Perdón. It's a local favourite, and many recipes are Moorish influenced. Dine on the top-floor terrace for views of the mosque.

🕐 Last admission is 30 minutes before closing, but try to allow at least an hour to do the site justice.

• Calle Torrijos, Córdoba
• Map D3
• 957 47 05 12
• www.turismo decordoba.org
• Open Mar–Oct: 10am–6:30pm Mon–Sat (Apr–Jun: to 7pm); Nov–Feb: 10am–5:30pm Mon–Sat (Jan & Dec: to 5pm). Also open 9–10:15am and 2–7pm Sun & hols. 1 Jan, 24, 25 & 31 Dec: 10am–2pm.
• Adm €8.00

Top 10 Features

1. The Caliphal Style
2. Puerta del Perdón
3. Patio de los Naranjos
4. Torre del Alminar
5. Interior
6. Recycled Columns
7. Mihrab
8. Capilla de Villaviciosa & Capilla Real
9. Cathedral
10. Choir Stalls

1 The Caliphal Style

The mosque was begun by Caliph Abd el-Rahman I in AD 786. La Mezquita constitutes the beginning of the Caliphal architectural style, combining Roman, Gothic, Byzantine, Syrian and Persian elements.

2 Puerta del Perdón

Originally entrance to the mosque was gained via many doors, also designed to let in light. This door *(above)*, the Gate of Forgiveness (1377), is in Mudéjar style and is now the only one open to the public.

3 Patio de los Naranjos

The delightful Courtyard of the Orange Trees *(below)* would have been used by worshippers to perform ritual ablutions before prayer.

Torre del Alminar
A minaret once stood where the belfry now is. Built in 957, it was enveloped in this Baroque belltower *(above)*.

Interior
The plan of the interior is that of a so-called "forest" mosque, with the rows and rows of variegated columns (856 remaining) and arches said to evoke date palms. Unlike Christian churches, based on earlier Roman basilicas with their focus on the central enthroned "judge", the Islamic aim is to induce an expansive, meditative state for prayer.

6 Recycled Columns
Great ingenuity was required to achieve the rhythmic uniformity inside, since most of the columns used in construction were recycled from Roman, Visigothic and other sources. They were a hotchpotch of varying sizes, so the longer ones had to be sunk into the floor. To reach the desired height, a second tier was added.

7 Mihrab
Dating from the 10th century, this is the jewel of the mosque *(left)*. An octagonal chamber set into the wall, it was to be the sacred focal point of prayer, directed towards Mecca. No amount of ornamentation was spared. Emperor Nicephorus III sent artisans from Constantinople to create some of the finest Byzantine mosaics in existence.

8 Capilla de Villaviciosa & Capilla Real
One of the happier Christian additions, the Villaviciosa Chapel *(above)* has exuberant arches in the Mudéjar style and dates from 1377. Next to it, the Royal Chapel sports appealing Mudéjar stucco work and *azulejo* (tile) decoration.

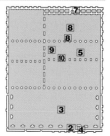

Plan of La Mezquita

9 Cathedral
In 1523 some 60 of the 1,013 columns were removed from the heart of the mosque and others walled up so as to construct the cathedral.

10 Choir Stalls
The Baroque choir stalls *(above)* date from 1758, and the exquisite carved mahogany depicts Biblical scenes.

A Spiritual Site
This magnificent edifice was not the first religious structure to be built on this spot. The Caliph bought the land from the Christians, who had built the Visigothic Cathedral of St Vincent here. In its last years, that building had been divided by a partition, so that it could serve the needs of Christian and Muslim communities. The Visigothic structure, in its turn, had been constructed on top of a Roman temple, and its columns are still visible in La Mezquita.

🔟 Cádiz

Glowing white in the intense southern light, Cádiz inspired the poet Lord Byron to praise its heavenly blue setting, gorgeous women and sensuous lifestyle. Nowadays it is one of Andalucía's under-visited treasures. According to ancient chronicles, it was founded by the Phoenicians as Gadir ("Fortress") in 1104 BC, giving it a good claim to being Europe's oldest city. Under the Romans it became Gades and was notable as the city where Julius Caesar held his first public office. Having been almost completely destroyed by an Anglo-Dutch raid in 1596, the old part of the present city is pure 18th-century and has remained virtually unchanged since then.

Barrio del Pópulo

🍽 **El Faro** *(see p107)* is the place to go for first-class seafood.

🎭 You must book up to a year ahead for accommodation during Carnaval.

• Map B5
• *Catedral Nueva: Plaza Catedral; 956 28 61 54; Open 10am–6:30pm daily (to 4:30pm Sat, from 1pm Sun); Adm €4.00; Torre de Poniente: Open 10am–6pm daily (mid-Jun–mid-Sep: to 8pm); Adm €3.50*
• *Torre Tavira: C/Marqués del Real Tesoro 10; 956 21 29 10; Open 10am–6pm daily (Jun–Sep: to 8pm); Adm €4.00*
• *Hospital de Mujeres: C/Hospital de Mujeres; 956 22 36 47; Closed for renovation*
• *Museo de Cádiz: Plaza Mina; 956 20 33 68; Open 9am–8:30pm Tue–Sat (from 2:30pm Tue), 9:30am–2:30pm Sun; Adm €1.50 (free for EU members)*

Top 10 Sights

1. Barrio del Pópulo
2. Plaza San Juan de Dios
3. Catedral Nueva
4. Iglesia de Santa Cruz & Teatro Romano
5. Plaza de la Flores
6. Torre Tavira
7. Hospital de Mujeres
8. Museo de las Cortes de Cádiz
9. Oratorio de la Santa Cueva
10. Museo de Cádiz

1 Barrio del Pópulo
The Barrio del Pópulo is the medieval heart of the city, which still retains its three 13th-century gates. The main entrance of what's left of the 18th-century city wall, the Puerta de Tierra *(above)*, marks the boundary between the old city and modern-day Cádiz.

2 Plaza San Juan de Dios
On the edge of the Barrio del Pópulo is this palm-fringed plaza *(right)*, dating from the 16th century. Facing the port, it forms the hub of city life.

3 Catedral Nueva
The "New Cathedral" *(above)* was begun in 1722. The belltower, or Torre de Poniente (western tower), offers superb views of the city below.

4 Iglesia de Santa Cruz & Teatro Romano
In the midst of the Barrio del Pópulo is this church dating from 1260 and the ruins of a Roman theatre.

Plaza de las Flores

This bustling market square *(above)* is also known as the Plaza de Topete – named after the tophet, a type of ancient Phoenician temple, that once stood here.

Map of Cádiz

Museo de Cádiz

Archaeological finds and Baroque paintings *(above)* are the museum's forte. Exhibits include a pair of 5th-century BC Phoenician marble sarcophagi, one male and one female, showing Greek and Egyptian influences; Roman shipwreck finds; and works by Zurbarán, Murillo and others.

Torre Tavira

The highest tower in the city *(below)* offers great views from its 46 m (150 ft) height.

Hospital de Mujeres

This Baroque former hospital's main attraction is the chapel's painting of the *Extasis de San Francisco* by El Greco.

Museo de las Cortes de Cádiz

A mural in this museum eulogizes Cádiz as the birthplace of liberalism. On 29 March 1812 Spain's first liberal constitution was conceived here, a document that played a major role in shaping modern European politics. The museum is currently closed for renovation.

Oratorio de la Santa Cueva

This elliptical Neo-Classical chapel has an upper church with an elegant dome supported by Ionic columns. Three frescoes by Goya depict miraculous moments from the life of Christ.

Los Carnavales

The vibrant Carnaval celebrations in this port town are the most exhilarating in all of Spain *(see p60)*. In fact, so dear is this annual blow-out to *gaditanos* (as the locals call themselves), that it was the only such event in the country that Franco's forces failed to suppress during the decades of dictatorship. The festival's various traditions date back to the 15th century, when the town had a significant Genoese enclave, though some claim there is also a strong Cuban influence.

The Torre Tavira sports Spain's first camera obscura, which projects live images of the city onto a large screen.

TOP 10 Ronda

This is the most famous of the pueblos blancos (white towns) – a scattering of evocative hamlets that reveal their Moorish roots between Málaga, Algeciras and Seville (see p96). Ronda is in the southwest corner of this zone and the only town in the wildly mountainous region of the Serranía de Ronda. Located just half an hour's drive from the Costa del Sol, Ronda hosts up to 75,000 tourists per day, yet has managed to retain its timelessness and charm, despite the inevitable modernization of recent decades. Its natural setting is so spectacular that the views alone make it a must-see experience.

Puente Nuevo

- Map D5
- www.turismoderonda. es
- Casa del Rey Moro: C/Santo Domingo 9; 952 18 72 00; Open (gardens only) 10am–7pm daily; Adm €4.00; Not recommended for those with limited mobility (200+ stairs)
- Baños Árabes: Barrio de Padre Jesús; 952 87 08 18; Open 10am–7pm Mon–Fri, 10am–3pm Sat & Sun; Adm €3.00
- Museo del Bandolero: C/Armiñán 65; 952 87 77 85; Open 10:30am–8:30pm daily; Adm €3.00
- Iglesia de Santa María la Mayor: Plaza Duquesa de Parcent; 952 87 40 48; Open 10am–8pm daily (Nov–Mar: to 6pm); Closed 2–4pm Sun; Adm €4.00
- Palacio de Mondragón: Plaza de Mondragón; 952 87 08 18; Open Mar–Oct: 10am–7pm Mon–Fri, 10am–3pm Sat & Sun; Adm €3.00
- Plaza de Toros: C/Virgen de la Paz 15; 952 87 41 32; www. rmcr.org; Open 10am–8pm daily; Adm €6.00

Top 10 Sights

1. El Tajo & Puente Nuevo
2. Casa del Rey Moro
3. Palacio del Marqués de Salvatierra
4. Puente Viejo & Puente de San Miguel
5. Baños Árabes
6. Minarete del San Sebastián
7. Museo del Bandolero
8. Iglesia de Santa María la Mayor
9. Palacio de Mondragón
10. Plaza de Toros

1 El Tajo & Puente Nuevo

Ronda perches upon a sheer outcrop that is split by a precipitous cleft, El Tajo, 100 m (330 ft) deep *(right)*. The spectacular 18th-century Puente Nuevo bridge links the old city, La Ciudad, with the commercial district.

2 Casa del Rey Moro

A visit to the gardens of this 18th-century mansion *(below)*, built on the foundations of a Moorish palace, will provide wonderful views.

3 Palacio del Marqués de Salvatierra

This 18th-century mansion is closed to the public, but its

façade sports a carved stone portal. The upper section features four squat figures *(left)* that may represent South American Indians.

4 Puente Viejo & Puente de San Miguel

The Puente Viejo (Old Bridge) dates from 1616 and is thought to be a rebuilding of a Roman span, though some say its pedigree is Moorish, like the Puente de San Miguel. Both cross the gorge at the upstream end of the Río Guadalevín.

The best views of the town and its stunning setting are from the road from Algeciras or the one from San Pedro de Alcántara.

Baños Árabes
5 These wonderfully preserved Moorish baths date from the 1200s or early 1300s. The multiple barrel vaulting pierced with star-shaped lunettes is typical of such structures, but the beautifully designed octagonal brick columns supporting horseshoe arches are highly original.

Iglesia de Santa María la Mayor
8 Much of this church incorporates a 13th-century mosque, notably the base of the Mudéjar belfry *(above)*.

Map of Ronda

Plaza de Toros
10 Inaugurated in 1785, Ronda's bullring was constructed in limestone in an elegant double-tiered sweep; it is the widest in the world and one of the oldest in Spain. Since Ronda is the birthplace of the sport, this is the spiritual home of the tradition. It also houses a museum about the bullfight.

The Origins of Bullfighting

The establishment here of the Real Maestranza de Caballería (Royal Academy of Knights) in 1572 set the stage for the birth of bullfighting as we know it. The Maestranza's role was equestrian-training of Spain's aristocracy and students would challenge wild bulls on horseback. Legend relates that when one rider fell from his horse and was attacked by a bull, a bystander distracted the animal by waving his hat. The man's grandson Pedro Romero (1754–1839) perfected the Ronda School of bullfighting. Ronda stages only a few fights a year, but they are the most prestigious.

Palacio de Mondragón
9 One of Ronda's most beautiful palaces *(below)* dates from 1314. Some of the original polychrome mosaic work and a magnificent Mudéjar ceiling can still be seen, but the rest was altered by the Christian overlords. Part of the palace is now the city's archaeological museum.

Minarete de San Sebastián
6 This graceful 14th-century tower *(above)* is all that remains of a Nasrid mosque.

Museo del Bandolero
7 For some 1,000 years, the Sierras were the haunt of bands of rebels and outlaws. The museum chronicles the history of such notorious brigands.

In early September, Las Corridas Goyescas are held in Ronda, in which matadors fight in costumes based on Goya's etchings.

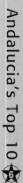

🔟 Costa del Sol

The former fishing villages of the "Sun Coast" welcome millions of international visitors each year – not counting the estimated 300,000 expats who call the coast home. The winning formula is 320 sunny days a year, warm, clean waters and beaches, and good-value, though somewhat brash, entertainment options. Heavy on neon and tower blocks, most of what's here has little to do with local culture, but what is exuberantly Andalucían is the verve with which visitors enjoy themselves in the sun. Nights, too, are given over to typically Spanish merriment that continues until dawn.

Málaga Old Town

🌀 Note that most sights and many shops close for the siesta from about 1pm to 5pm.

- *Estepona: Map D5; Tourist Office: Avda San Lorenzo 1; 952 80 09 13*
- *Marbella: Map D5; Tourist Office: Glorieta de la Fontanilla s/n; 952 86 89 77*
- *Mijas: Map D5; Tourist Office: Plaza Virgen de la Peña; 952 58 90 34*
- *Fuengirola: Map D5; Tourist Office: Avda Jesús Santos Rein 6; 952 46 74 57*
- *Benalmádena: Map D5; Tourist Office: Avda Antonio Machado 10; 952 44 24 94*
- *Torremolinos: Map E5; Tourist Office; Plaza Blas Infante 1; 952 37 95 12*
- *Málaga: Map E5; Tourist Office: Pasaje de Chinitas 4; 951 30 89 11*
- *Vélez-Málaga: Map E5*
- *Nerja: Map E5; Tourist Office: C/Puerta del Mar 2; 952 52 15 31*

Top 10 Towns

1. Estepona
2. Marbella
3. Mijas
4. Fuengirola
5. Benalmádena
6. Torremolinos
7. Málaga
8. Torre del Mar
9. Vélez-Málaga
10. Nerja

1 Estepona
The first major resort on this coast is an excellent quieter choice, with 19 km (12 miles) of beach *(right)*. In the *casco antiguo* (old town), Plaza Las Flores *(below)* retains considerable charm.

3 Mijas
Come here for the views of the coast, as well as the maze of old Moorish streets filled with charming shops in the numerous tiny squares.

2 Marbella
The 15th-century Plaza de los Naranjos is the heart of the old town of Marbella, Spain's most expensive resort. Nearby Puerto Banús is the town's glittering marina *(right)*, where you can admire the fabulous yachts and breathe the same air as the super-rich.

4 Fuengirola
This large resort is the most family-orientated, with a good beach and a seafront promenade. There is a restored 10th-century Moorish castle overlooking the town.

Estepona still has a large fishing fleet, with a fish auction every dawn when the boats come in with their catch.

Benalmádena
This resort comes in three parts: the old town inland; the beach and port area *(above)*; and Arroyo de la Miel, a lively suburb.

Map of Costa del Sol

Vélez-Málaga
The old quarter of this market town *(below)* has beautiful Mudéjar features. An annual flamenco guitar competition is held here every July.

Nerja
No high-rises here; Nerja is all white-washed good taste, surmounting attractive, verdant cliffs with quiet pebble beach coves below.

Franco's Costa Dream

It was General Franco, Spain's dictator until 1975, who had the idea of transforming this impoverished zone of fishing villages into the "Florida of Europe". He implemented his plan in the 1960s with money loaned by the US, in return for the right to build nuclear bases on Spanish soil. The jet-set glamour and cheap package deals were a runaway success, so much so that by the 1970s the area was an aesthetic and environmental disaster – with added corruption and organized crime. Since the 1980s, steps have been taken to clean up all these issues.

Torremolinos
Torre de los Molinos (Tower of the Windmills) refers to a Moorish watchtower that was at one time surrounded by 19 flourmills. The ancient Torre Vigia is still here, but surrounding it now is a big, brash and trashily modern resort that is the quintessence of inexpensive fun *(below)*.

Málaga
Málaga is mostly a transit point for the average visitor and thus remains very Spanish in character. Andalucía's second largest city has an interesting historic district dominated by a vast 8th-century fortress and the ruins of the 14th-century Castillo de Gibralfaro *(see p96)*.

Torre del Mar
This resort is favoured by Spanish families, so is less tawdry than others to the west. The tree-lined seafront promenade is part of an attempt to prettify facilities.

For places to eat and to party on the Costa del Sol **See pp104–5**

27

Baeza and Úbeda

These two Jaén Province towns, only 9 km (5.5 miles) apart, are like matching jewel boxes overflowing with Renaissance architectural treasure, and so were awarded the title of UNESCO Word Heritage Sites in 2003. Of the two, quiet Baeza has managed to stay almost completely out of the modern age, while Úbeda has a thriving new zone and even some light industry. Nevertheless, its stunning historic district is, if anything, even more spectacular than Baeza's.

Plaza Santa María, Baeza

⭐ Baeza's Restaurante Andrés de Vandelvira *(see p123)* is situated in a restored convent, making it a very special treat. In Úbeda, enjoy a drink in the courtyard of the fabulous Parador Condestable Dávalos *(see p140).*

✆ The Úbeda potters are all located along Calle Valencia; look for the workshops of the premier ceramists, the Tito family.

• Baeza: Map F2; Tourist Information Office: Casa del Pópulo, Plaza del Pópulo; 953 74 04 44; www.todosobrebaeza.com; Open 8:30am–2:30pm & 4–6pm (5–7pm summer) Mon–Fri, 10am–2pm Sat, 10am–1pm Sun
• Úbeda: Map F2; Tourist Information Office: Palacio del Marqués de Contadero, C/Baja del Marqués 4; 953 75 55 21; www.ubedainteresa.com; Open 8am–3pm & 4–7pm (5–8pm summer) Mon–Fri, 10am–2pm Sat & Sun

Top 10 Sights

1. Puerta de Jaén, Baeza
2. Plaza del Pópulo, Baeza
3. Plaza Santa María & Catedral, Baeza
4. Palacio de Jabalquinto, Baeza
5. Paseo de la Constitución, Baeza
6. Plaza de Vázquez de Molina, Úbeda
7. Plaza del Primero de Mayo, Úbeda
8. The Pottery Quarter, Úbeda
9. Plaza San Pedro, Úbeda
10. Plaza San Lorenzo, Úbeda

1 Puerta de Jaén, Baeza

This section of the ancient wall, the Jaén Gate *(above)*, supports an additional arch with coats-of-arms set above.

2 Plaza del Pópulo, Baeza

The town's most charming area, the Plaza del Pópulo, is surrounded by Renaissance edifices. It is also called the Square of the Lions, after its fountain, which sports four stone lions and a female figure *(right)*.

3 Plaza Santa María & Catedral, Baeza

This square is fronted by several glorious 16th-century structures, including the cathedral. One of the many masterpieces by Renaissance architect Andrés de Vandelvira, it was originally a Gothic church, built over a mosque in the 13th century.

Palacio de Jabalquinto, Baeza

One of the most unusually decorated palaces in town is the 15th-century Palacio de Jabalquinto *(right)*. Its façade is sprinkled with coats of arms and stone studs in Isabelline Plateresque style.

Plaza San Pedro, Úbeda

Visit the patio of the Real Monasterio de Santa Clara, the town's oldest church, where the sisters will sell you their distinctly Arabic *dulces* (sweetcakes). The Palacio de la Rambla is another graceful Vandelvira creation and is now home to a small luxury hotel *(see p143)*.

Plaza San Lorenzo, Úbeda

The Casa de las Torres has a Plateresque façade *(above)*, flanked by two vast square towers and with gargoyles on the cornice. The Church of San Lorenzo is unique in that its façade is on the parapet of the old wall.

Paseo de la Constitución, Baeza

Here the 16th-century Alhóndiga (Corn Exchange) has an elegant façade with three-tiered arches, while the Torre de los Aliatares is an ancient remnant of the old wall.

Plaza de Vázquez de Molina, Úbeda

In this square *(above)* the Capilla del Salvador, built by Vandelvira, marks a high point in the Spanish Renaissance.

Plaza del Primero de Mayo, Úbeda

The variety of riches here includes the Iglesia de San Pablo *(above)*, displaying an array of styles, the 15th-century Casa Mudéjar, now an archaeological museum, and the 16th-century Ayuntamiento Viejo, with its superb arcades.

The Pottery Quarter, Úbeda

Passing through the Puerta del Losal, a splendid 13th-century Mudéjar gate, takes you into the town's age-old pottery quarter. Ceramic artists renowned all over Spain and beyond ply their ancient trade here.

Architecture of the Spanish Renaissance

Spanish Renaissance architecture divides into three periods: Plateresque, Classical High Renaissance and Herrerean. The first refers to the carved detailing on silverwork (*platero* means silversmith), a carry-over from the late Gothic style popular under Queen Isabel (Isabelline Plateresque). The High Renaissance style is noted for its symmetry and its Greco-Roman imagery. Herrerean works are very sobre, practically devoid of decoration.

Typical Úbeda pottery is glossy forest green decorated with piercings reminiscent of Moorish patterns **See p122**

🔟 Parque Nacional del Coto Doñana

The largest nature reserve in Europe and southern Spain's only national park was established in 1969. It covers more than 247,000 acres, including its surrounding buffer zones, and its wide variety of ecosystems, rare fauna and abundance of bird life make it so vital to the environmental stability of Western Europe that it enjoys the status of a UNESCO Biosphere Reserve. To the untrained eye, it yields up its natural wonders gradually, but a visit to the coastal area of western Andalucía is not complete without taking it in.

Birdlife on the wetlands

🍴 The main visitor centre has an acceptable snack bar.

✈ Bring binoculars, mosquito repellent, sunscreen and comfortable walking shoes – and watch out for quicksand.

If you join in the Romería del Rocío, you will also need your own sleeping bag, water and food.

• Map B4 • www.
turismodedonana.com;
Reservations 959 44 87
11 • Open 8am–7pm
daily (summer: to 9pm);
Tours 8:30am & 5pm
(summer), 8:30am & 3pm
(winter) • Adm €23.00
• Centro de Visitantes
El Acebuche: Ctra A483,
3 km (2 miles) from
Matalascañas;
959 44 87 11
• Centro de Información
La Rocina; 959 44 23 40;
Open 9am–7pm daily
(summer: 10am–3pm &
4–8pm)
• El Rocío Turismo:
Avda de la Canaliega;
959 44 38 08

Top 10 Features

1. Setting and History
2. Habitats
3. Flora
4. Fauna
5. Visitor Centres
6. Guided Tours
7. Bird Shelter
8. Huts
9. El Palacio de Acebrón
10. El Rocío's Romería

1. Setting and History

Located at the estuary of the Guadalquivir River, the area probably owes its present pristine condition to the fact that it was set aside as a hunting preserve for the nobility in the 16th century.

2. Habitats

The park comprises three distinct types of ecosystem: dunes, *coto* (pine and cork forests and scrubland) and *marisma* (wetlands). The wetlands *(below)* can be broken down into marshes, salt marshes, lagoons and seasonally flooded areas.

3. Flora

Umbrella pines and cork-oaks flourish here and both types of tree provide crucial nesting sites for many birds. Wildflowers in the dunes and scrubland areas include the bright pink spiny-leafed thrift, besom heath, yellow gorse and the bubil lily. Marshland vegetation is made up of bullrushes, other types of reeds and white-flowered buttercups.

➡ *Access to the park is strictly controlled, but there are a limited number of marked footpaths along its borders.*

4 Fauna

The endangered pardel lynx *(below)* is the emblem of the park. As many as 25 pairs of the very rare Iberian eagle also survive here. Other birds include the rare purple gallinule and the flamingo, but at least 300,000 birds make their home in the park.

6 Guided Tours

Tours in all-terrain vehicles *(above)* depart from the Visitor Centres. Two visits per day have varying itineraries, depending on the time of year. The marshes dry up in the summer months, which limits birdwatching, but increases the chance of seeing rare mammals.

7 Bird Shelter

The Centro de Visitantes El Acebuche, the main visitor centre, is set on a lagoon. At the eastern end there is an aviary where rescued and recuperating birds get intensive care. It's an opportunity for visitors to view them – including some unusual species – fairly close-up.

5 Visitor Centres

Several Visitor Centres offer exhibitions as well as planned trails which lead to bird-watching opportunites *(below)* and rest areas.

8 Huts

Dating from the 18th century, these traditional huts *(above)* are found in the *pinares* (pine forests). Sometimes clustered into small villages, the uninhabited structures are pinewood frames covered with local thatch.

9 El Palacio de Acebrón

This Neo-Classical style hunting lodge, built in 1961, has a permanent exhibition on the history and ethnography of the region. There are good views from the upper floors and the site is a starting point for a 12-km (8-mile) trail through the nearby woodlands.

10 El Rocío's Romería

This town *(see p87)* is the focal point of one of Spain's largest festivals, the Romería del Rocío. The four-day pilgrimage leading up to Whitsun has dispensation to wind its way through the park *(below)*. Thousands of people come to honour Nuestra Señora del Rocío, a medieval statue with miraculous powers.

Ecological Issues

Despite vigilant efforts to protect the park, in 1998 a Río Tinto mining toxic waste storage burst, dumping pollutants into the Guadiamar River, one of the wetlands' main tributaries. Thankfully, the poisonous wave of acids and heavy metals was stopped just short of the park, but damage was done to its border areas. Although the ramifications are now under control, the clean-up continues.

Booking guided tours in advance is essential, as each 4-hour trip is limited to about 20 participants.

🔟 The Sierra Nevada

The Sierra Nevada ("Snowy Mountains") include Spain's tallest peaks and are Europe's second-highest mountain range after the Alps. Until the 20th century, their only regular visitors were the so-called neveros ("icemen"), who brought back blocks of ice to sell in nearby Granada, and for many years the only part they played in a tour of the region was as the glistening backdrop to the Alhambra Palace. But in recent decades they have become more and more popular in their own right – for trekking, skiing and exploring the remarkable collection of villages on their southern slopes, Las Alpujarras.

Sierra Nevada mountains

⊖ Lovers of *jamón serrano* (mountain ham) must not fail to try the snow-cured version from the town of Trevélez *(see p65).*

⊘ Extra sun protection is vital here, particularly for skiers. Hikers and trekkers should have good walking shoes, something to wear against the wind, water, some food and binoculars.

Petrol stations are a rarity in Las Alpujarras. Coming from the west, Órgiva is a good place to fill up.

• Map F4
• Parque Nacional de la Sierra Nevada: Ctra Antigua de Sierra Nevada, km 7; 958 02 63 00; www.redde parquesnacionales. mma.es (in Spanish)
• Sierra Nevada Club (skiing): Plaza de Andalucía, Solynieve; 902 70 89 00; www. sierranevadaski.com

Top 10 Features

1. Setting
2. Flora & Fauna
3. Hiking
4. Skiing
5. Puerto del Suspiro del Moro
6. Las Alpujarras
7. Valle de Lecrín
8. Lanjarón
9. Órgiva
10. Barranco de Poqueira

Setting
This mountain chain and its national park are home to Spain's highest peak, Mulhacén (3,482 m/11,425 ft) at the western end and fertile valleys to the south.

Flora & Fauna
Snow-capped most of the year, these heights are nevertheless rich in wildflowers. Some 60 varieties are unique here, including a giant honeysuckle. The ibex is the most common species of fauna, but there are also butterflies, and birds such as the golden eagle.

Snow-capped Sierra Nevada

Hiking
There is a paved road over the top of the range but the uppermost reaches have been closed to cars since the national park was established in 1999. In summer it's a hiker's paradise – the second highest peak Veleta (3470 m/ 11,385 ft) is a relatively easy 5-hour roundtrip.

Skiing
The main ski resort, Solynieve, is Europe's highest and most southerly, in operation from December to April or even May. The pistes and facilities *(left)* are good enough to have hosted the world Alpine skiing championships in 1996.

5 Puerto del Suspiro del Moro

Heading south from Granada on the N323, you'll come to the spot known as the "Pass of the Moor's Sigh". Here, bereft Moorish ruler Boabdil (see p35), expelled by the Christians, is said to have looked back on his beloved city for the last time.

7 Valle de Lecrín

This bucolic valley is filled with olive, almond and citrus groves – the almond blossom is stunning in late winter.

9 Órgiva

Made the regional capital in 1839, this town (left) remains the area's largest. It's at its best on Thursday mornings, when everyone comes alive for market day, and you can find traditional local products such as hand-woven rugs.

10 Barranco de Poqueira

This vast and gorgeous ravine (above) is home to a stunning collection of tiny villages. Much loved by visitors seeking tranquillity, the remote site even boasts its own Tibetan Monastery, founded in 1982. The ravine is an excellent place for easy day walks, and each town offers traditional local crafts.

8 Lanjarón

Famous since Roman times for its curative mineral springs, the town (below) is now a modern balneario (spa) and marks the beginning of the Alpujarras proper. Below the long main street you'll find a ruined Moorish castle, from which the views across the gorge are breathtaking.

6 Las Alpujarras

On the southern side of the Sierra Nevada is this dramatic zone, home to a stunning series of white villages (above). The architecture here is pure Moorish, almost identical to that found in the Rif Mountains of Morocco. Houses are flat-roofed, untiled, clustered together and joined by neighbourly bridges.

Brenan's South from Granada

In the 1920s British writer Gerald Brenan, a member of the Bloomsbury set, came to live in the village of Yegen in the eastern Alpujarras. A plaque in the town marks the house he lived in. He recorded his experiences in his book *South from Granada*, a wonderful evocation of the place and its people, whose way of life still prevails largely unchanged. The 2002 Spanish film *Al Sur de Granada*, based on the book, is a true and delightful dramatization of his story.

Left **Moorish fort** Right **Discovery of America**

Moments in History

1 Bronze Age Developments

The Iberian (Tartessian) civilization got its strongest start around 2500 BC when bronze began to be smelted and worked in Andalucía. Some early tribes built the oldest megalithic tombs *(dolmens)* in western Europe.

2 Phoenician and Greek Colonies

Attracted by the area's mineral wealth, the Phoenicians founded a trading post at what is now Cádiz in 1100 BC, while the Greeks established a toehold near Málaga in 636 BC. The two maintained a mercantile rivalry until Carthage, a former Phoenician colony, dominated the region.

3 Roman Spain

The first Roman town in Spain, Itálica *(see p89)*, was established in 206 BC; Rome finally wrested the entire region from the Carthaginians in 201 BC. Due to abundant local produce, Andalucía became one of the empire's wealthiest outposts.

Andalucian Roman ruins

4 Arab Domination

Some 700 years later, when the Roman Empire began to come apart, tribes from northern Europe laid claim to the peninsula. The Vandals and then the Visigoths ruled for some three centuries. Politically unstable, a question of rightful succession in AD 710 led to the enlistment of Muslim armies from North Africa. The Moors saw their chance and within 10 years had taken over.

5 Moorish Sophistication

The Moors were custodians of the best features of Roman civilization: religious tolerance, scientific and philosophical thought, and engineering and cultural refinements *(see pp34–5)*. In the 10th century, under the Caliphate of Abd ar-Rahman III, Córdoba became the largest and wealthiest city in Europe.

6 Reconquista

The dissolution of the Caliphate in 1031 marked the beginning of the end for Moorish Spain. Some 30 *taifas* (principalities), jostling for political hegemony, proved no contest for the Christians. The eight-month siege and *reconquista* of Granada in 1492 was the most poignant loss.

7 Discovery of America

That same year the New World was discovered for Spain by Christopher Columbus. The result was a wealth of gold and silver from the new empire.

Imperial Collapse

8 Colonial losses that began in 1713 following the War of Spanish Succession reached their *dénouement* with Spain's defeat in the Spanish-American War of 1898. In Andalucía this long decline meant grinding poverty and mass emigration.

Civil War and Franco

9 The Spanish Civil War (1936–9) was ignited by a military coup led by General Francisco Franco, who was against Spain's continuance as a Republic. On 18 July 1936 the war began when they took Cádiz, Seville and Granada. Then followed the grim years (1939–75) of Franco's repressive dictatorship.

Seville Expo '92

10 The world fair in 1992 celebrated the quincentenary of Columbus's discovery of the New World. It brought a sprucing up of Seville and 42.5 million visitors to Andalucía, but it left bankruptcy in its wake. The scale of the economic disaster was political; charges of corruption led to a loosening of the Socialist Party's hold on power, in favour of a right-wing government.

Pabellón de Andalucía, Seville Expo '92

Top 10 Historic Andalucían Figures

1 Melkarth
The Phoenician's name for Hercules, whom legend claims to have founded Andalucía.

2 Trajan
One of the greatest Roman emperors (AD 98–117) was a native of Itálica.

3 Hadrian
Trajan's successor (117–38) was a great builder, emphasizing Rome's Classical Greek roots.

4 Abd el-Rahman III
The Syrian leader (912–61) established the autonomous Caliphate of al-Andalus.

5 Boabdil
The final Moorish ruler (r.1482–92) lost Granada to the Catholic Monarchs.

6 Isabel and Fernando
Isabel of Castilla and Fernando of Aragón (1479–1516) were dubbed "The Catholic Monarchs".

7 Christopher Columbus
The Genoese sea captain (1451–1506) set sail from Huelva Province and, on 12 October 1492, landed on one of the Bahamian islands.

8 Emperor Carlos V
His reign (1516–56) left Spain nearly bankrupt, but with cultural legacies such as his palace in Granada *(see p9)*.

9 Felipe V
Felipe V (1700–46) had his court in Seville until a claim to the throne by Archduke Charles of Austria led to the War of Spanish Succession.

10 Felipe González
A native of Seville, this left-wing leader (1982–96) brought rapid change to Spain and to Andalucía, which was given relative autonomy.

Left **Horseshoe arches, Moorish architecture** Right **Moorish ceramic azulejo tile**

Aspects of Moorish Heritage

1 Art and Architecture
Moorish art and architecture is full of signs and symbols and often incorporates calligraphy into its designs, quoting the Koran or poetry. The point was to inspire the viewer to reflect upon the unity of all things under Allah, whose power and perfection could never be equalled by the achievements of man.

2 Religious Tolerance
Although non-Muslims had to pay a special tax and wear distinctive clothing, Moorish policies towards Jews and Catholics were generally easygoing. There was greater repression after the fundamentalist Almohads came into power in the 12th century, but on the whole the faiths were well integrated for centuries.

3 Music
The Moors can be credited with the development of the guitar, which they adapted from the four-stringed lute. The Middle Eastern musical forms they imported were also to have an effect later on flamenco *(see pp58–9)*.

4 Gardens
Moorish gardens make prominent use of water – so important to people from a perpetually arid land. It was sprayed, channelled, made to gurgle and fall, to please the ear and eye. Jasmine, honeysuckle and roses are just a few of the flowers the Moors brought to the region.

5 Agriculture
Inheriting many of their techniques from the Romans, the Moors were masters of agricultural engineering. Their system consisted of three main elements: the aqueduct, the waterwheel and the irrigation channel. Thereby, they were able to cultivate vast areas, often building ingenious terracing on slopes. They also introduced many crops, including bitter oranges, lemons, almonds, rice, cotton, pomegranates, aubergines (eggplants), artichokes, asparagus and mulberry trees (to feed silk-worms).

6 Philosophy
Great minds of Andalucía, such as the Moor Averroës and the Jew Maimonides, were considered among the most advanced thinkers of their age. The former almost single-handedly preserved the writings of Aristotle, while the latter's writings sought to reconcile Biblical faith and reason.

Moorish garden, Generalife

7 Science

Moorish scientists excelled in the fields of metallurgy, zoology, botany, medicine and mathematics. Moorish inventors also developed revolutionary devices such as the astrolabe and the quadrant, essential for navigation. Arabic numerals were introduced, as well as algebra (from *al-jebr*, meaning "reuniting broken parts") and the algorithm.

8 Food

The simple fare that had existed prior to the Moorish incursion – centred around olives, wheat and grapes – gave way to a bounty of flavours. Almonds, saffron, nutmeg, pepper and other spices became commonplace in the region.

Almonds

9 Language

Modern Spanish is full of everyday terms that come from Moorish heritage – the word for "left" *(izquierda)* is almost pure Arabic and any word beginning with the prefix *al-* (the) comes from Arabic too.

10 Crafts

The hand-tooled leather of Córdoba, silver and gold filigree jewellery, pottery, silk and embroidered goods, and inlaid creations all owe their existence to the Moors' 800-year hegemony.

Top 10 Moorish Sites

1 Moorish Granada

The spectacular Alhambra palace is the gem of Spain's Moorish heritage, while the adjacent Generalife offers sumptuous gardens *(see pp8–11).*

2 Real Alcázar, Seville

The front towers and gateway of Seville's royal palace retain their Moorish origins *(see pp14–15).*

3 La Mezquita, Córdoba

This vast mosque marked the beginning of the Arab-Hispanic style known as Caliphal *(see pp20–21).*

4 Baños Arabes, Ronda

These Moorish baths feature horseshoe arches, typical of Arabic architecture *(see pp24–5).*

5 Medina Azahara, Córdoba

Sadly now in ruins, this one-time splendid palace epitomized the city's glory in the 10th century *(see p119).*

6 Almonaster La Real

The village's mosque is one of Andalucía's finest, with great views from the minaret *(see p90).*

7 Alcazaba, Almería

One of the largest surviving fortresses in the region *(see p111).*

8 Alcazaba, Málaga

Remains of the original Moorish walls and tower can still be seen *(see p96).*

9 Las Alpujarras

The villages on the slopes of the Sierra Nevada retain distinctive Moorish architecture *(see pp32–3).*

10 Vejer de la Frontera

The most Moorish of the *pueblos blancos (see p42).*

Left **Fortaleza de la Mota, Alcalá la Real** Right **Castillo de Vélez Blanco**

🔟 Alcázares, Palacios and Castillos

1 Real Alcázar, Seville
This sumptuous palace and extensive gardens constitute a world of royal luxury. The architectural styles are a blend of mainly Moorish traditions – note the lavish use of the horseshoe arch, glazed tilework and wood ceilings *(see pp16–17)*.

2 La Casa de Pilatos, Seville
Few palaces are more opulent than this 15th–16th-century mansion. A mix of Mudéjar (Christian-Islamic), Flamboyant Gothic and Renaissance styles, it is also adorned with Classical sculptures, including a 5th-century BC Greek Athena and important Roman works. A noble residence to this day, it is filled with family portraits and antiques from the last 500 years *(see p75)*.

Roman relief, Casa de Pilatos

3 Ayuntamiento, Seville
Seville's town hall dates from the 16th century, with later modifications added in the 19th century. The original sections are in Plateresque style, begun by architect Diego de Riaño in 1526 – note the mix of motifs used on the main façade (on Plaza de San Francisco). Inside, a collection of art features paintings by Zurbarán and Velázquez *(see p76)*.

4 Palacio del Marqués de la Gomera, Osuna
This 18th-century palace is a striking example of the Spanish Baroque style. The cornice is composed of waves and volutes, lending it a sense of movement. The family escutcheon crowns the carved stone doorway, which also has elaborate pillars. The palace has now been converted into a hotel and restaurant. ◈ C/ San Pedro 20, 954 81 22 23 • Map D4

5 Fortaleza de la Mota, Alcalá la Real
This Moorish castle, crowning the hill above the town, is the chief attraction here. Created by Granada's rulers in the 14th century, it incorporates 12th-century structures and earlier elements, since the strategically situated town dates from pre-historic times. After the Christian reconquest in 1341 *(see p32)*, additions to the fortress continued until the 16th century. The castle keep houses an archaeological museum *(see p122)*.

Castillo de Santa Catalina, Jaén City

Restored by the Christians, this 13th-century castle towers above the town and affords spectacular views. ◈ Map F3 • Open 10am–2pm, 5–9pm Tue–Sun (summer); 10am–2pm, 3:30–7:30pm Tue–Sun (winter) • 953 12 07 33 • Adm

Castillo de La Calahorra

Castillo de Burgalimar, Baños de la Encina

This Moorish castle is one of the best preserved in Andalucía. Its horseshoe-arched main gate bears an inscription dating its construction to AD 967. Some 14 square towers provide vistas far and wide. ◈ Map F2 • Visit by appt, 953 61 32 00 • Free

Palacio de Jabalquinto, Baeza

This splendid 15th-century palace is a study in originality. The façade's columns defy categorization, while the gallery evokes the Renaissance style, as does the double-tiered patio. The latter also sports a monumental Baroque staircase (see p29).

Castillo de La Calahorra

One of the few castles newly built after the Christian reconquest, this was also one of the first in Spain to be built according to Italian Renaissance tenets. Despite its forbidding situation and exterior, its inner courtyard is exquisite, with staircases, pillars and arches carved from Carrara marble. ◈ Map F4 • Open 10am–1pm, 4–6pm Wed • 958 07 71 32 • Free

Castillo de Vélez Blanco

In Italian Renaissance style, this structure has the grace of a fairytale castle. Unfortunately, it was gutted in the early 1900s, but a reconstruction of one of the patios gives you some idea of its original splendour. ◈ Map H3 • Open 10am–2pm & 4–6pm (Apr–Sep: 5–8pm) Wed–Sun • 607 41 50 55 • Free

Visit www.castillosybatallas.com for a programme of festivities (medieval festivals, markets etc) at Jaén's castle grounds.

Left **Arches, La Mezquita** Right **Retablo Mayor, Seville Cathedral**

🔟 Places of Worship

Seville Cathedral
Seville's most striking architectural masterpiece is its vast cathedral. Inside are soaring columns, precious artworks and the world's largest altarpiece *(see pp14–15)*.

La Mezquita, Córdoba
This spectacular mosque may have been savagely reconsecrated but visitors can still see its Byzantine mosaics and other exquisite marvels *(see pp20–21)*.

Mosque, Almonaster la Real
Virtually unchanged for 1,000 years, this is one of the few surviving rural mosques in Andalucía and has the oldest *mihrab* (Mecca-facing prayer niche) in Spain *(see p90)*. ✪ Map B3 • Open 10am–7:30pm daily; Ayuntamiento 959 14 30 03 • Free

Oratorio de San Felipe Neri, Cádiz
As the commemorative plaques adorning the façade reveal, this fine Baroque church is one of the most significant buildings in Spain – and not simply due to its unusual elliptical floorplan. On 29 March 1812 a group of Spanish patriots defied a Napoleonic blockade and met here to compose the country's first constitution. The document's liberal ideas have inspired fledgling democracies ever since. ✪ Plaza San Felipe Neri • Map B5 • Open 10am–1pm Mon–Sat; 956 21 16 12 • Adm

La Colegiata de Santa María de la Asunción, Osuna
From its hilltop, this massive Spanish Renaissance church dominates the town. Its austere façade is relieved by a fine Plateresque portal, the Puerta del Sol. Inside, treasures include five masterpieces by José de Ribera, a Crucifixion sculpture by Juan de Mesa, beautiful Renaissance ornamentation and a wonderfully high-spirited Baroque altarpiece *(see p88)*.

Iglesia de San Mateo, Lucena
It's intriguing to find one of the masterpieces of Andalucían Rococo design in this industrial town – especially because Lucena was famous for having been a virtually independent Jewish enclave during Moorish rule. The gem of this 15th-century church is its 18th-century octagonal sacristy and the complex decoration of the chapel and its dome. ✪ Map E3 • Open during services • Free

Plaques, Oratorio de San Felipe Neri

If visiting places of worship during services, be as courteously unobtrusive as possible and avoid wearing skimpy clothing.

7 Capilla Real and Catedral, Granada

Although not without aesthetic merit, these two structures are more about Christian triumph and royal ego than they are about spirituality. At the Royal Chapel's sarcophagi, note how Queen Isabel's head presses more deeply into her marble pillow than that of King Fernando – said to indicate greater intelligence In the cathedral is the equestrian statue of El Matamoros ("The Killer of Moors") by Alonso de Mena *(see p109)*.

8 Monasterio de San Jerónimo, Granada

This Renaissance magnum opus is largely the creation of Diego de Siloé, one of the great masters of the age. The façade's upper window is flanked by sinuous mythological animals and medallions. Inside, the altar is complex and monumental, consisting of row upon row of high reliefs framed by columns.
Ⓝ C/Rector López Argueta 9 • Map F4
• Open Apr–Oct: 10am–2:30pm & 4–7:30pm daily; Nov–Mar: 10am–2:30pm & 3–6:30pm daily; 958 27 93 37 • Adm

Catedral, Granada

Catedral de Jaén

9 Catedral de Jaén

The cathedral was primarily the work of famed Renaissance architect Andrés de Vandelvira, although the west façade was designed later, decorated with Baroque sculptures by Pedro Roldán. Every Friday between 11:30am and 12:45pm, one of Spain's holiest relics, the Reliquía del Santo Rostro de Cristo, is brought out for the faithful to kiss. It is believed to be the cloth that St Veronica used to wipe Christ's face on the road to Calvary. An impression of the holy face is said to have been miraculously left upon it *(see p121)*.

10 Capilla del Salvador, Úbeda

Designed by Siloé and Vandelvira, this masterpiece of Andalucían Renaissance was commissioned as a family pantheon and is still privately owned. The sacristy is the highlight, employing caryatids and atlantes as columns and pilasters. It was once embellished by a Michelangelo sculpture, a sad casualty of the Spanish Civil War *(see p29)*.

Left **La Iruela, outside Cazorla** Right **Zahara de la Sierra**

🔟 Villages

1 Almonaster La Real

From a distance, this lovely *pueblo blanco* in Huelva Province looks like a sprinkling of snow amid the green of the surrounding forests. The citadel features one of the oldest mosques in the region, dating from the 10th century *(see p90)*.

2 Alájar

Another pretty Huelva Province village, where the stone houses seem ageless. There are some nice Baroque churches too. More intriguing, however, is the mystical importance of the place, as seen in the hallowed caves and hermitage on the cliff above the town *(see p90)*.

3 El Rocío

Deserted most of the year except for the handful of residents – who still customarily get around on horseback – this town fills up to overflowing with as many as one million pilgrims during the annual Romería *(see p31)*. It's worth a visit at any time, however, to take in its wonderful Wild West-style architecture, as well as to book a tour of the nearby Coto de Doñana nature reserve *(see p87)*.

4 Vejer de la Frontera

This inland village in Cádiz Province probably retains its quintessential Moorishness more than any other town in Andalucía. It stands gleaming white on a hill with a view of the coast, and its warren of maze-like alleys and byways is virtually indistinguishable from any North African town. Before the Spanish Civil War, women here wore a traditional veiled garment like the Muslim *heshab*, called the *cobijado*; now they are only worn during August festival *(see p99)*.

5 Arcos de la Frontera

The historic part of this town is from the Cuesta de Belén to the Puerta de Matrera – a zone that has been a recognized national monument since 1962. Consequently, it is beautifully preserved. Central to the area is the Plaza del Cabildo, with ancient walls in evidence and set about with orange trees. Unfortunately the castle below the square is not open to the public, but the terrace of the parador opposite is a fine place for a drink with a view *(see p98)*.

Church, El Rocío

Gothic-Mudéjar church, Arcos de la Frontera

Zahara de la Sierra

The town's name means "flower" in Arabic and this quiet little hamlet lives up to its implications. Scented with orange groves, it's a delight to see on the approach and offers equally fine views once there. The ruined castle, however, stands witness to tougher times. In the 15th century it was attacked continually, sought by both Muslims and Christians for its position guarding the northern access route to the Serranía de Ronda. ✆ *Map C4*

Sabiote

This hamlet is a hidden gem. It boasts a Roman pedigree, its medieval walls are largely intact, and it has one of the most impressive castles in the region – Moorish in origin but restored by the famed architect Andrés de Vandelvira, who was born here. He also designed several mansions for local nobility. ✆ *Map F2*

Iznatoraf

This mountain eyrie of a place opens out onto 360-degree panoramas of the Cazorla highland. The best view is from the mirador above the cliff at the village's northern edge. ✆ *Map F2*

Cazorla

Simple whitewashed cubes cluster around a citadel here, while birds of prey overhead remind you that this is the southwestern entrance to the Sierra de Cazorla *(see p44)*. The town's position made it a prize for Moors and Christians, hence the castle in town and the ruined La Iruela, 1 km (0.5 miles) away. ✆ *Map G3*

Castril

At the foot of an imposing stone outcropping and surrounded by the Parque Natural de la Sierra de Castril, this enchanting town dates back to Roman times. The parish church dominates the upper reaches, while down below there surges a mountain torrent. ✆ *Map G3*

Left **Parque Nacional del Coto Doñana** Right **Sierra de Aracena**

🔟 **Nature Reserves**

1 Parque Nacional del Coto de Doñana
These important floodplains are a UNESCO Biospheric Reserve and have been a national park since 1969. The ecosystems include sand dunes, pine and cork forests, marshes, scrubland and riverbank. More than six million birds stop here on their annual migrations and fauna includes the last of the Iberian lynx population *(see pp30–31)*.

2 Sierra Nevada
Spain's highest mountains and Europe's southernmost ski resort can be found in this national park. It's a wonderful area for hiking, horse-riding and mountain biking *(see pp32–3)*.

3 Sierra de Aracena y Picos de Aroche Park
This part of the Sierra Morena in Huelva Province is very rural in character; traditions cling tighter here, notably the culinary techniques that give rise to its world-famous ham, *jamón ibérico*.

Again, these forested hills lend themselves to exploration on foot or horseback *(see p90)*.

4 Sierra Norte
Sevilla Province's northern reaches are wild and beautiful. In fact, hiking is a better option than driving in many cases, due to rough, pot-holed roads. The area is a great choice for outdoor enthusiasts of any sort – anglers, hunters and climbers are in their element here. 🚉 *Map C3*

5 Parque Natural de la Sierra de Cardeña y Montoro
This beautiful park is home to prolific forests of holm oak, cork and pine. For the most part gently rolling, it gives way to more dramatic topography in the west. There are plenty of marked hiking trails, and it's a good place for spotting local fauna. 🚉 *Map E2*

6 Sierra de Cazorla
In eastern Jaén Province, this vast and enormously diverse park is home to some 1,300 known species of flora, including 20 that are unique to the zone. Steep cliffs, deep gorges and an intricate pattern of rivers, lakes and streams typify the terrain. The landscape offers plenty of walking opportunities along marked trails. 🚉 *Map G2*

Sierra Nevada

Cabo de Gata-Níjar

Cabo de Gata-Níjar

7 In Almería Province a stretch of pristine coastline has been set aside as a nature reserve, with towering rocks setting off beaches and coves. The semi-desert massif was designated a UNESCO Biosphere Reserve in 1997. The zone is excellent for scuba-diving *(see p49)*. ◈ *Map H4*

Sierra de Grazalema

8 Some 132,200 acres of verdant wilderness were designated a UNESCO Biosphere Reserve in 1984. Access is strictly controlled and is only possible on foot. ◈ *Map C5*

El Torcal

9 Málaga Province's most dramatic natural sight is this limestone massif, carved by the weather over countless millennia into bizarre forms. It's a popular destination for hikers and climbers. ◈ *Map D4*

Parque Natural de los Montes de Málaga

10 Most of this park was planted to cloak Málaga's once barren heights so as to prevent the seasonal flooding the city experienced for several centuries. Just 30-minutes' drive from town, it's a fine place for hiking and biking, with colour-coded trails taking you through a land of gorges, forests and valleys. ◈ *Map E5*

Top 10 Flora and Fauna

1 Trees
These include black and umbrella pine, holm oak, hazel, olive, citrus, cypress, juniper, ash and the rare Spanish fir.

2 Shrubs
Along the coast you'll see agave, brought here from America in the 18th century. Also prickly pear, bullrush, club rush, oleander and arbutus.

3 Wildflowers
Look for the Cazorla violet, bubil lily, Nevada daffodil and white celandine.

4 Raptors
Birds of prey include the Spanish imperial eagle and the peregrine falcon.

5 Songbirds
Warblers include the red-legged partridge, collared pratincole and hoopoe.

6 Marsh birds
Watery areas abound in cranes, flamingo, gull-billed terns, purple gallinules, stilts, glossy ibis and redshanks.

7 Mammals
Wild creatures include wolves, lynxes, boar, genets, civets, mongoose, monk seal, dolphins, whales and the Barbary macaques of Gibraltar.

8 Reptiles and Amphibians
This group includes the Montpellier snake, the Spanish lizard and the natterjack toad.

9 Fish
Local catch includes black perch, eel, gambusia, tuna, monkfish, sardines, anchovies and cephalopods.

10 Insects and Arachnids
Most of Europe's butterflies are found here, along with mosquitoes, scorpions and tarantulas.

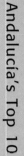

There is a 1.5-km (1-mile) trail around El Torcal called the Ruta Verde, or book a guided tour (Antequera Tourist Office: 952 70 25 05).

Left **Parque de María Luisa** Right **Parque Genovés**

🔟 Paseos, Plazas, Parks and Gardens

1 Parque de María Luisa, Seville

Seville's glorious main park was a gift to the city from a Bourbon duchess in 1893. A few decades later it was redesigned and embellished for the 1929 Ibero-American Exhibition. Numerous lavish structures have been left behind, including the stunning Plaza de España and several other fine buildings, now used mostly as cultural centres. The grounds are largely the creation of Jean-Claude Nicolas Forestier, the French landscape gardener who also designed the Bois de Boulogne in Paris (see p79).

2 Paseo Marqués de Contadero, Seville

This central promenade is one of Seville's loveliest. Stretching along the riverfront, within sight of most of the major monuments, its tree-lined walkways make a pleasant break from the crowded city streets. The *paseo* is also pedestrianized so you don't have to worry about traffic (see p79).

Paseo de Marqués de Contadero

3 Parque Zoológico, Jerez

Jerez's small zoo, set in botanical gardens, is also an active centre for the rehabilitation of regional endangered species or any injured animals. The star turns are a pair of white tigers. This is also the only chance you may get to see the elusive and extremely rare Iberian lynx, of which only an estimated 1,000 remain in the wild. ✪ C/Taxdirt • Map B5 • Open 10am–6pm Tue–Sun (May–Sep: to 7pm); 956 14 97 85 • www.zoobotanicojerez.com • Adm

4 Parque Genovés, Cádiz

Lying along the west side of Cádiz, this swathe of landscaped greenery facing the seafront has paths for strolling along, some civic sculpture and interesting flora, including an ancient dragon tree originally from the Canary Islands. This is one leg of a two-part park, the other half curving around along the northern seafront. ✪ Map B5

5 Plaza San Juan de Dios, Cádiz

This is one of Cádiz's busiest hubs of commercial and social life. Lined with cafés, bars and palm trees, its chief adornment is the monumental Neo-Classical façade of the Ayuntamiento (town hall), along with several handsome towers. The square opens out onto the port, ensuring a constant stream of pedestrians and opportunities for people-watching. ✪ Map B5

6 Jardín Botánico La Concepción, Málaga

Just north of Málaga City lies this impressive botanical garden, the work of a 19th-century English woman, Amalia Livermore, and her Spanish husband, Jorge Loring Oyarzábal. The garden houses a collection of palms and exotic plants from around the world. The grounds are also embellished with charming touches here and there, such as a domed gazebo decorated with tiles and columns. ◈ *Carretera N-331, km 166, Málaga • Map E5 • Open 9:30am–5:30pm Tue–Sun (Apr–Sep: to 8:30pm); 952 25 21 48 • www.laconcepcion.ayto-malaga.es • Adm*

7 Plaza de la Corredera, Córdoba

Córdoba gave this 17th-century arcaded square a long overdue sprucing up for the tourist onslaught of 1992 *(see p33)*, even putting in an underground car park. But it still retains some of its customary functions, including an open-air market on Saturday morning, in addition to the regular covered market in the building with the clock-tower. The arches provide shade for a number of cafés and *tapas* bars, where you can sit and admire the brick façades with their wrought-iron balconies. ◈ *Map D3*

Plaza de la Corredera

8 Alcázar de los Reyes Cristianos, Córdoba

Another of the major delights of Córdoba are the grounds of this palace *(see p18)*. The gardens are lavishly done in Moorish style, indulging in a profusion of colour – wisteria, bougainvillea, calla lilies and geraniums, to name only a few – gorgeously setting off the sun-bleached stone walls and ancient carvings. ◈ *Campo Santo de los Mártires • Map D3 • Open Tue–Sun • Adm €4.00 (free Fri)*

Plaza Nueva

9 Plaza Nueva, Granada

Located at the base of both the Alhambra hill and the Albaicín *(see pp8–13)*, and providing views along the banks of the river that runs beneath the city, this is a great place to while away the time. There are street performers, an endless stream of people and plenty of cafés with tables on terraces. ◈ *Map Q2*

10 Paseo de la Constitución, Baeza

Baeza's hub for strollers and café-goers is all along this oblong central promenade. Fountains grace its tree-lined length, and there are bars with open-air seating in the shade. Interesting buildings facing the square include La Alhóndiga, the old corn exchange, with its triple-tiered arches *(see p29)*. ◈ *Map F2*

Left **Cabo de Gata** Right **Marbella**

⓾ Beaches

1 Ayamonte

Andalucía's westernmost town is located at the mouth of Río Guadiana, and just to the east are the beach resorts Isla Canela and Isla Cristina. Isla Canela has a long, broad beach and a laidback array of bars and bungalows, while Isla Cristina boasts a fine sandy stretch and an attractive harbour. ◈ Map A4

Mazagón

2 Mazagón

Huelva Province's Costa de la Luz has several appealingly remote beaches, and Mazagón is one of them. Located 23 km (14 miles) southeast of Huelva City, this low-key resort is surrounded by pines and has lovely dune beaches. Deserted in winter, it comes alive in summer, mostly with Spanish families, but there's plenty of empty expanse to find solitude. ◈ Map B4

3 Chipiona

Cádiz Province has some very special beach resorts that lack the high tourism of further along the coast, and Chipiona is one of the nicest. The beaches are excellent and, as an added plus, the town has retained its age-old traditions. It's still a thriving fishing port, for example, as well as a renowned producer of the local sweet muscatel wine. In addition, historic attractions include the longest jetty in the Guadalquivir estuary, known as Turris Caepionis to the Romans and these days as Torre Scipio *(see p99)*. ◈ Map B5

4 Tarifa

Cádiz Province's – and Europe's – southernmost point is one of the best spots in the world for devotees of the West Wind. The wind practically never ceases blowing here, which makes it a top beach for wind-surfers and the like, but some-thing of a misery for sunbathers. Still, it is possible to find protect-ed niches that shelter you from the wind, and the nightlife and sense of fun here are second to none *(see p99)*. ◈ Map C6

Windsurfers, Tarifa

Marbella

The Costa del Sol's smartest town naturally has several fine beaches to recommend. To the east there are Cabo Pino, a nudist beach, and Las Dunas, sand dunes beside a modern marina. To the west is a string of party beaches, good for barbecues and dancing, including Victor's Beach and Don Carlos, perhaps Marbella's best *(see p26).* ✎ *Map D5*

Torremolinos

Considering that they are in the main Costa del Sol nightlife magnet, Torremolinos's beaches come as a pleasant surprise. Because of the steep streets, most of the action remains above as you make your way down to the sand *(see p27).* ✎ *Map E5*

Torre del Mar

Very much off the beaten Costa del Sol track, this area – frequented mostly by local Spanish families – has quite a bit going for it if you want a more low-key time *(see p27).* ✎ *Map E5*

Nerja

This little town is a favourite for those who want an alternative to the brash Costa del Sol. It's a welcoming spot, with a wonderful position on top of an imposing cliff and palm-fringed beaches down below *(see p27).* ✎ *Map E5*

Nerja

Almuñécar

The main resort on the Costa Tropical of Granada Province is a more relaxed alternative to the intensity of the Costa del Sol. The two central beaches are the Playa San Cristóbal and the Playa Puerto del Mar, separated by a headland. Good diving and windsurfing spots can be found along here *(see p110).* ✎ *Map F5*

Cabo de Gata

Almería Province offers some of the finest unspoilt beaches in the region, centred on this natural park. The main resort town is San José, and from here you can walk to a number of perfect finds, including the Cala de la Media Luna and the Playa de Mónsul *(see p45).* ✎ *Map H5*

Left **Costa del Sol marina** Right **Mountain horse-riding**

Outdoor Activities and Sports

1 Diving
Off Gibraltar you can check out the many sunken ships, while the wilds around Cabo de Gata offer the most profuse underwater life. The Costa de la Luz also has some good spots, including watersport heaven, Tarifa. *Centro de Buceo Isub: C/Babor, San José; Map H5; 950 38 00 04; www.isubsanjose.com • Yellow Sub Tarifa: C/Covadonga 4, Tarifa; Map C6; 956 68 06 80; www.divingtarifa.com*

2 Windsurfing and Surfing
Thanks to the constant winds, Tarifa is a magnet for windsurfers, while good possibilities also can be found along the Costa Tropical. For board surfing, the Costa de la Luz provides sufficiently high waves. Mediterranean waves are only good for body-surfing. *Club Mistral: Hurricane Hotel, Ctra N340 km 78, Tarifa; Map C6; 956 68 49 19 • Windsurf La Herradura: Paseo Marítimo 34, La Herradura; Map F5; 958 64 01 43*

Windsurfer, Costa Tropical

3 Horse-riding
Andalucía is renowned for breeding very fine horses and offers a range of riding options, with trails and schools in every province. *Camino Verde, Cortijo El Sabuco 18416, Busquistar; Map F4; 958 85 89 47; www.caminoverde.co.uk • Rancho Los Lobos: Estación de Jimena, nr Jimena de la Frontera; Map C5; 956 64 04 29; www.rancholoslobos.com*

4 Hiking
Andalucía is blessed with sierras in which to hike, from verdant, to desert-like, to rocky *(see pp44–5)*. If mountaineering appeals, head for the Sierra Nevada. Maps and lists of refuges are available from the Federación Española de Deportes de Montaña (FEDME). *FEDME • 958 29 13 40 • www.fedme.es*

5 Spelunking
The region is home to some of the world's most interesting caves, many of them commercially developed. For information and organized jaunts, contact Ticket-to-Ride. *Ticket-to-Ride: Avda Naciones Unidas Centro Commercial Cristamar B61, Puerto Banús, Marbella • Map D5 • 952 90 50 82*

6 Skiing
The resort near Granada, Solynieve, is the only possibility in Andalucía. Although a little too sleek compared to its Alpine cousins, it offers a variety of runs and, best of all, skiing fairly late in the season *(see p33)*.

The entire coast is great for general swimming, with many blue-flag (safe) waters on the Costa del Sol.

7 Boating and Fishing

With so many marinas along the coast, sailing is big here. For deep-sea fishing, you need a five-year licence; for freshwater fishing, you'll need a two-week licence. *Spanish Fishing Federation: C/León Felipe 2, Almería; 950 15 17 46 • Spanish Sailing Federation: Avda Libertad, Puerto de Santa María (Cádiz); 956 85 48 13*

Costa del Sol golf course

8 Golf

So copious are the golf courses that the Costa del Sol has often been dubbed the "Costa del Golf". Courses include everything from world masterpieces, designed by top golfers, to putting greens *(see p103)*.

9 Fútbol

Football (soccer) is a national obsession, stirring up the deepest of passions. In season, you'll encounter it in every bar, blaring out from the TV.

10 Bullfighting

In the Spanish view, this is not really a sport, but an art form, and to many Andalucíans, it embodies the soul of the region. The fight season runs from April to October and tickets are available from bullrings.

Top 10 Aspects of Bullfighting

1 History
The bullfight may have roots in primordial religions involving bull sacrifice.

2 Scheduling
There are about 500 bullfights each year in Spain, usually as part of a festival.

3 The Fight
Usually three groups fight two bulls each. Each of the six confrontations is a drama in several acts, called *tercios*.

4 Cast of Characters
The fight *(corrida)* begins with a procession of all the bullfighters.

5 Picadores
In the first *tercio* the matador taunts the bull with a red cape. The picadors goad the bull on horseback with steel-pointed lances to weaken the animal's powerful drive.

6 Banderilleros
Next the *banderilleros* enter on foot, sticking pairs of spikes in his back, to provoke the bull further into a frenzy.

7 Matador
In the final *tercio* the matador makes passes with the *muleta* cape, bringing the fight to its climax.

8 The Kill
This ideally amounts to a quick thrust of the sword, straight to the heart.

9 Post Mortem
Matadors are idolized in Spain, and the crowd jeers when his job is done and the bull's corpse is dragged away.

10 Celebration
At the end of the fight, a band plays, roses are tossed, hankies are waved, and the matador may be carried out on his men's shoulders.

Left **Guadalquivir Valley** Right **Southern Tahá**

🔟 Hikes and Drives

1 Hike from Alájar to Linares de la Sierra

The Sierra de Aracena is defined by soaring cliffs, wooded valleys and whitewashed villages. A good hike along the marked trails is the 6-km (4-mile) route from Alájar to Linares, via the hamlet of Los Madroñeros. It begins at the main square in Alájar and follows the old road, with only one steep section. ◈ *Map B3*

2 Río Borosa Hike

From the visitors' centre at the village of Torre del Vinagre, near Cazorla, this hike takes you along the narrow rock walls of the Cerrada de Elías gorge above the Río Borosa, criss-crossed by wooden bridges. ◈ *Map G3*

3 Hike around the Villages of the Southern Tahá

This hike begins in Pitres and descends south, to arrive first at Mecinilla, then along a ravine to Mecina-Fondales. From here, you take the short or long route to Ferreirola, climb up to Atalbéitar and then back to Pitres. ◈ *Map F4*

4 Hike from Rute to Iznájar

Leave Rute on the A331 south, veer left at the fork and then take the trail on the right about 500 m (550 yd) further on. This leads down to the reservoir; turn right and continue to a rocky promontory. Enjoy the views, then go up the hill and cross the bridge to the scenic village of Iznájar. ◈ *Map E4*

5 Serranía de Ronda Hike

An easy, picturesque hike connects the village of Benaoján Estación with Jimera de Líbar Estación. Begin at the Molino del Santo hotel, walk down the hill and left along the railway and then over at the second crossing. Across the river is the path; when it divides, take the left fork and continue on to Vía Pecuaria and into the town. ◈ *Map D5*

Drive from Nerja to Almería

6 Drive from Nerja to Almería

A route along some of the region's most panoramic coastline. Nerja is built up on cliffs *(see p27)*, and as you approach Almería City the views are dramatic *(see p111)*. ◈ *Map E5 • Rte N340*

7 Drive from Ronda to Jerez

The attraction of this drive is the *pueblos blancos (see p96)* along the way, in particular Grazalema, Zahara and Arcos de la Frontera. You can also include the Roman ruins at Ronda la Vieja, and a sidetrip to Olvera. ◈ *Map C5 • Rte N342*

➡ *Marked hiking trails are called* senderos *in Spanish.*

Andalucía's Top 10

Drive from Tarifa to Cádiz

8 This wild sweep of the Costa de la Luz *(see p98)* is the best of the Atlantic shore. Expect immense cliffs, mammoth sand dunes and a scattering of rather subdued resorts. The villages of Bolonia, with its ancient Roman sites, and Vejer de la Frontera, which is steeped in Moorish heritage, both make excellent sidetrips. ⊗ *Map C6 • Rte N340*

Drive from Guadalquivir Valley through Córdoba Province

9 Starting to the east of Córdoba, in the attractive hill town of Montoro, this drive follows the river downstream. West of Córdoba, visit the once-fabulous Medina Azahara *(see p119)*, enjoy the view from the castle walls at Almodóvar del Río, and end at Palma del Río. ⊗ *Map D3*

Drive in Las Alpujarras, Sierra Nevada

10 This zone comprises scores of villages and hamlets, many perched on the slopes of the Sierra Nevada. Begin at Lanjarón, then head for the market town of Órgiva. Continuing eastward, the landscape becomes more arid; eventually you'll come to Yegen, made famous by Gerald Brenan's autobiographical *South from Granada*. ⊗ *Map F4*

Sierra Nevada road

Top 10 Town and City Walks

1 Seville
Once you've done the main city-centre sights, head across the Puente de Isabel II and into the old gypsy quarter of Triana *(see pp74–7)*.

2 Granada
Lose yourself in the maze of hilly streets in the Albaicín district *(see pp12–13)*.

3 Córdoba
Have a free-form wander around the ancient Jewish quarter and then make for the Puente Romano for sunset views *(see pp18–21)*.

4 Cádiz
Start at the northeast corner of Plaza de España and circumambulate the city, taking in the seascapes and gardens *(see pp22–3)*.

5 Jerez
Stroll through the Barrio de Santiago, the town's gypsy quarter *(see p98)*.

6 Ronda
Cross the Puente Nuevo, turn left and follow the town clockwise, being sure to pass the main church *(see pp24–5)*.

7 Baeza
From Plaza del Pópulo most of the main sights are found in a counterclockwise direction *(see pp28–9)*.

8 Úbeda
Take a westerly walk to the monumental Hospital de Santiago and the Plaza de Toros *(see pp28–9)*.

9 Málaga
Málaga's historic sights are on the north side of the Paseo del Parque *(see p96)*.

10 Antequera
This ancient town's main attractions are located at the foot of the Alcazaba *(see p96)*.

⊗ *Some of these hikes can be steep but none of them requires anything more than general fitness. Carry water with you.*

53

Left **La Maestranza façade** Right **Archivo de las Indias**

Museums and Galleries

1 Museo de Bellas Artes, Seville

Housed in an exquisite former convent, this art museum is second only to Madrid's famed Prado. Paintings include early works by Velázquez, important works by Zurbarán, Ribera, El Greco, Murillo, Valdés Leal and Vásquez *(see p75)*.

2 Archivo de Indias, La Lonja, Seville

This museum is a vast archive given over to the discovery and conquest of the New World; four centuries of Spanish empire are painstakingly catalogued. The museum is housed in an 18th-century edifice that was built as the merchants' exchange *(see p78)*. The building and the archive are registered as a World Heritage Site by UNESCO.

Museo de Bellas Artes

3 Museo de la Maestranza, Seville

One of the corridors of what is perhaps Spain's most famous bullring is devoted to a Museo Taurino (Museum of the Bullfight). In addition to stacks of posters and other memorabilia, you can see the *trajes de luces* (suits of lights) – brightly coloured silk outfits embroidered with gold sequins – worn by many a celebrated toreador, along with portraits of some of the greats. There are also the inevitable stuffed remains of various noble animals *(see p78)*.

4 Museo de Cádiz

A Neo-Classical mansion houses Cádiz's main museum, a rich juxtaposition of archaeological treasures and fine art. In Europe's oldest city there are naturally artifacts from ancient cultures, including jewellery, pottery and small bronzes, but most notably a pair of 5th-century BC marble sarcophagi. Among the art are works by Zurbarán, Rubens, Murillo and Cano. An ethnological collection features artisanal pieces that highlight aspects of the city's culture *(see p23)*.

5 Museo del Bandolero, Ronda

This offbeat museum celebrates the story and legend of the Serranía's famous bandits and highwaymen. They were mostly active in the 19th century and

Visit the official website for Andalucía's most important museums at www.juntadeandalucia.es/cultura/museos

managed to capture the imagination of many writers of the period, who portrayed them as romantic figures living a devil-may-care life in communion with nature. As the exhibits here will attest, they were anything but "diamonds in the rough" *(see p25)*.

Museo del Bandolero

that do, however, are the life-size 1st-century AD Roman bronze representing a naked young man, possibly Ganymede, cupbearer to the gods, and a life-like carving of St Francis of Assisi, executed in wood by Pedro de Mena, a 17th-century Andalucían master *(see p96)*.

6 Museo Arqueológico, Córdoba

A small 16th century Renaissance mansion is home to this excellent collection, essential for understanding the city's importance in Roman times. In fact, the mansion was built over a Roman structure and there is an ancient patio to prove it. A sculpture of the Persian god Mithras, from a mithraeum found at Cabra, is particularly fine. Other parts of the collection focus on Iberian finds and Moorish artifacts *(see p19)*.

7 Museo Municipal, Antequera

This museum is located in a striking 18th-century ducal palace, which means that many of the exhibits simply cannot compete with the context. Two

Museo Arqueológico, Córdoba

8 Museo Picasso, Málaga

Opened after years of planning and several setbacks, this is the world's third largest museum dedicated to the modern master. It was endowed by his daughter-in-law, Christine Ruiz Picasso, and her son Bernard with some 187 paintings, including some major canvases, that give an idea of the breadth and depth of his career *(see p96)*.

9 Museo Arqueológico Cueva de Siete Palacios, Almuñécar

This space was built into the side of the hill in the 1st century. The small collection includes artifacts from Phoenician, Roman and Moorish periods *(see p110)*.

10 Museo Provincial y de Bellas Artes, Jaén

The archaeological lower floor has an interesting assortment of finds, but the 5th-century BC Iberian stone sculptures are truly extraordinary. Found near the town of Porcuna, in the western part of the province, they show clear influences from Greek works. Upstairs, the fine arts museum has some fine medieval wood sculpture and a Picasso drawing *(see p121)*.

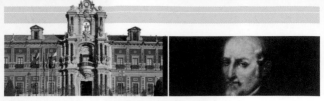

Left **Palacio de San Telmo façade by Figueroa** Right **Alonso Cano portrait**

🔟 Art and Culture

1 Andrés de Vandelvira
Andrés de Vandelvira (1509–75) was the quintessential architect of the Spanish Renaissance in Andalucía. His work spanned the three major phases of the style's predominance, from ornamental Plateresque, to Italianate Classical, to austere Herreran. He can be given virtually sole credit for the architectural treasures in the town of Úbeda and many important edifices in Baeza *(see pp28–9)*.

2 Francisco de Zurbarán
The great painter (1598–1664) spent most of his life in and around Seville, where his art adorns churches and museums. His works are noted for their mystical qualities, dramatized by striking *chiaroscuro* (light and shade) effects – hallmarks, as well, of his contemporaries Caravaggio and José de Ribera.

St Luke before Christ, Zurbarán

3 Velázquez
Born in Seville, Diego Rodríguez de Silva y Velázquez (1599–1660) left for Madrid in 1623 to become court painter to the king. His was the most remarkable talent of the golden age of Spanish painting, taking naturalism and technique to new heights. The works that remain in his home town were mostly religious commissions, although his real genius lay in portraiture.

4 Alonso Cano
Most of the works by Cano (1601–67) can be seen in Granada, largely because after he was accused of killing his wife the city vowed to protect him if he would work exclusively for them. Sadly, such a predicament limited the opportunities for this gifted painter, sculptor and architect to fully blossom.

5 Bartolomé Esteban Murillo
Murillo (1618–82) was the most successful of the Baroque painters from Seville. He received countless commissions to produce devotional works, notably the many *Immaculate Conceptions* seen in Andalucía.

6 Pedro Roldán
Roldán (1624–99) was one of the chief proponents of the Spanish aspiration to combine painting, sculpture and architecture into unified works of art, such as the altarpiece in Seville's Hospital de la Caridad *(see p78)*.

7 Leonardo de Figueroa

Figueroa (1650–1730) was a highly accomplished Baroque architect. His commissions in Seville included the Hospital de los Venerables *(see p76)*, the Palacio de San Telmo and the Museo de Bellas Artes *(see p73)*.

8 Manuel de Falla

Andalucían de Falla (1876–1946) was Spain's finest classical composer. One of his major works, *The Three-Cornered Hat*, has its roots deep in flamenco.

9 Pablo Picasso

Picasso (1881–1973) was born in Málaga, although he settled in France in 1909. His native land, with images of the bullfight and later of the horrors of the Franco era, turned up in his work throughout his career.

10 Federico García Lorca

The Granada born writer (1898–1936) was also an artist, musician, theatre director and more. Homosexual and Socialist too, he was murdered by Franco's Nationalists at the start of the Spanish Civil War. His work shows his love for Andalucían culture.

Portrait of Federico García Lorca

Top 10 Works Inspired by Andalucía

1 Lord Byron

The English Romantic poet's fascination with Andalucía is chronicled in his mock-epic poem *Don Juan* (1819).

2 Chateaubriand

The French writer's 1826 novel *The Last of the Abencerrages* was a bestseller.

3 Washington Irving

The American writer lived in Granada for some time and produced the hit *Tales from the Alhambra* (1832).

4 Théophile Gautier

The French writer's *Journey to Spain* (1841) gives a descriptive clarity to the region.

5 Calderón

This Málaga born writer's *Andalucían Scenes* (1847) featured the first ever description of a gypsy festival.

6 Opera

Operas set in Andalucía include *The Marriage of Figaro* (1786, Mozart), *The Barber of Seville* (1816, Rossini) and *Carmon* (1875, Bizet).

7 Manuel Machado

The works of Machado (1874–1947), such as *Cante Jondo*, evoke a poetic passion for Andalucía.

8 Dalí and Buñuel

This Surrealist pair created the shocking avant garde film *Un Chien d'Andalou* in 1928.

9 Ernest Hemingway

The American writer was a newspaper correspondent in Spain during the Civil War. *For Whom the Bell Tolls* is based on his Andalucían experiences.

10 Salman Rushdie

The Indian author's *The Moor's Last Sigh* (1995) was inspired by the exile of Granada's last Moorish king.

Left **Flamenco musicians** Centre **Guitar-maker** Right **Cave dwelling**

Aspects of Gypsy Culture

1 Origins
Gypsies *(Roma)* arrived in Eastern Europe in the 14th century and in Andalucía in the 15th century. Linguistic research shows that their language, Romany, was related to ancient dialects from northern India. Why they left India is unclear, but was possibly due to war with invading Muslims.

2 History
Although gypsies have remained outsiders throughout their history, they found a more congenial civilization in Andalucía than anywhere else. The culture was decidedly Middle Eastern and not dissimilar to that of their native land. With the Christian reconquest, however, "pagan" gypsies were forced into hiding or into further wanderings.

3 Song
Fortunately for Andalucían culture, many gypsies stayed, and eventually developed a unique strain of music, flamenco, drawing on Arabic, Jewish and Byzantine sources, as well as their own Indian traditions.

Similar to the American Blues, it is the raucous, rhythmic music of the dispossessed and marginalized, full of pathos and catharsis. The word flamenco is probably a corruption of the Arabic *felag mengu* (fugitive peasant), an epithet that 19th-century Andalucían gypsies used with one another.

4 Dance
Similarities between Middle Eastern and North African dance forms and flamenco are obvious. But using the feet to create rapid and complex staccato rhythms, combined with the expressive arm and hand gestures, clearly resembles traditional kathak dancing from northern India, confirming its true roots.

5 Guitar
The six-stringed flamenco guitar can be traced back to the medieval lute. Compared to the classical guitar, it is lighter, shallower and less resonant, so that it can be played extremely fast, and also features a thick plate below the soundhole for tapping out rhythms.

Gypsy singers

6 Flamenco Legends
A few of the names who advanced the art include: singers El Fillo and La Niña de los Peines; guitarist Paco de Lucía; and dancers La Macarrona and Carmen Amaya.

Sevillanas

This strident dance, with clapping rhythms, has been infused with the flamenco spirit. It is danced with enthusiasm at festivals throughout the region.

Horses

Andalucían gypsies have a reputation for their ability to train their steeds. To watch a gypsy horseman putting an animal through its paces is to witness an amazing display of communication between man and beast.

Gypsy horseman

Cave-dwellings

In remote hills and mountains gypsies escaped Christian persecution by turning caves into homes. Although flooding and other natural mishaps have decimated these communities in recent decades, many gypsies return to their former dwellings to perform lively and authentic flamenco shows for visitors.

Performances

Historically, flamenco is an improvised performance that arises spontaneously from a gathering, but the rule these days tends towards scheduled spectacles. Still, if the mood is right, these events still generate a great deal of emotion.

Top 10 Flamenco Venues

1 La Taberna Flamenca, Jerez

Flamboyant shows. ◈ *Callejón Angostillo de Santiago • Map B5 • 956 32 36 93*

2 La Bulería, Jerez

This club is named after a flamenco festival held in September. ◈ *C/Empedrada 20 • Map B5 • 956 05 37 72*

3 Sanlúcar de Barrameda

This town holds the Feria de Flamenco in July. ◈ *Map B5*

4 Juan Villar, Cádiz

A good *peña* for genuine flamenco. ◈ *Paseo Fernando Quiñones, Puerto la Caleta • Map B5 • Open Tue–Sun; 956 22 52 90*

5 El Arenal, Seville

First-class performances. ◈ *C/Rodo 7 • Map L4 • 954 21 64 92*

6 Casa de la Memoria de al-Andalus, Seville

Another museum, with performances *(see p83)*.

7 Tablao Flamenco Cardenal, Córdoba

Authentic shows. ◈ *C/Torrijos 10 • Map D3 • Open Mon–Sat; 957 48 31 12*

8 Venta El Gallo, Granada

Professional performances. ◈ *Barranco de los Negros 5 • Map F5 • 958 22 84 76*

9 La Peña Platería, Granada

One of Spain's oldest *peñas*. ◈ *Placeta de Toqueros 7 • Map F5 • 958 21 06 50*

10 Peña El Taranto, Almería

Named after the province's contribution to the genre, the *taranto* dance. ◈ *C/Tenor Iribarne 20 • Map G4 • 950 23 50 57 • www.eltaranto.net*

Granada's La Peña Platería is a private flamenco club but is sometimes open to the public. Telephone 958 21 06 50 for details.

Left **Carnaval, Cádiz** Right **Feria de Abril, Seville**

Religious Festivals

Fiesta de los Reyes Magos
Traditionally, this evening commemorates the arrival of the Three Kings at the infant Jesus's manger crib. Parades across the region feature the trio, lavishly dressed, progressing through towns in small carriages drawn by tractors or horses. The next day, Epiphany, is the day that children receive gifts. ✎ *5 Jan*

Carnaval
Most Andalucían towns celebrate this Catholic festival, the most spectacular extravaganza being in Cádiz. Costumes and masked balls and lots of carousing are the order of the day and night during these chaotic revels. The implicit anarchy invites every sort of political lampoon, which is why Franco tried to abolish these events – unsuccessfully *(see p23)*. ✎ *Feb*

Semana Santa
Holy Week is observed in every town and village in the region, with dramatic and spectacular processions,

Semana Santa procession

especially in Seville. Effigies of Christ and the Virgin are carried through the streets on huge floats, sometimes accompanied by music. The people, dressed in traditional outfits, either maintain penitential silence or express their commiseration with the suffering Lord and His mournful Mother *(see p15)*. ✎ *Easter week*

Corpus Christi
This festival celebrates the miracle of Transubstantiation, when the host becomes the body of Christ and the wine His blood. Granada's celebration is the most famous, with parades and partying, followed by bullfights and flamenco. ✎ *Dates vary*

Romerías
Taking part in one of these local festivals is an experience no visitor will forget – almost every community has its own *romería*. Usually, the programme involves a colourful pilgrimage to a shrine outside of town, followed by days of merrymaking. The name may recall ancient pilgrimages, when devotees walked to Rome *(see p31)*. ✎ *May–Oct*

Fiesta de las Cruces
The Festival of the Crosses celebrates the discovery of the True Cross in the 4th century by St Helena. Modes of veneration vary widely in the region, but may include competitions for producing the most gorgeous flower-decked cross. ✎ *3 May*

Romería celebrations

7 San Juan

This feast is important in many parts of Andalucía. In celebration of John the Baptist, midsummer fireworks and bonfires seem to be the rule in most communities. ◈ *23 & 24 Jun*

8 Virgen del Carmen

The patron of sailors is all-important in coastal communities. Statues of the Virgin are put onboard a decorated fishing boat and floated out to sea and back again, amid flowers, fireworks, music and cheering. Thus the waters are blessed for the coming year. ◈ *15 & 16 Jul*

9 Ascension of the Virgin

At the height of the summer heat, the day of the Virgin's ascension into heaven is celebrated. In colourful marquees there is much socializing, drinking and dancing. The day marks the beginning of the Feria de Málaga, a week-long festival. ◈ *15 Aug*

10 Fiesta de San Miguel

This mix of bullfights, exhibitions and dancing is particularly noteworthy in Seville, Úbeda and the Albaicín quarter of Granada. In Torremolinos it closes the summer season in festive style. ◈ *Last week Sep–first week Oct*

Top 10 Ferías and other Festivals

1 Flamenco Festivals

These take place during the summer months all around the region.

2 Moros y Cristianos

Festivals centre on re-enactments of Christian take-overs of various towns throughout the year.

3 Feria de Abril

Held in Seville two weeks after Easter, this is the largest fair in Spain *(see p76)*.

4 Feria del Caballo

This fair in Jerez de la Frontera centres on Andalucían horses. ◈ *May*

5 Music & Dance Festivals

The most famous of these takes place in Granada from late June to early July.

6 Wine Festivals

Celebrations of the fruit of the vine occur from April to September, when *La Vendimia* (grape harvest) takes place.

7 Sherry Festivals

The "Sherry Triangle" *(see p98)* celebrates their fortified wines at various times, notably in Jerez. ◈ *Sep–Oct*

8 Feria de Jamón

Late summer and autumn sees the traditional *matanza* (slaughter) of pigs and several celebrations of ham, notably in Trevélez. ◈ *15 Aug*

9 Fiesta de la Aceituna

The olive is celebrated in the Jaén province town of Martos. ◈ *1st week Dec*

10 Fiesta de los Verdiales

In Málaga Province at Puerta de la Torre, this is a day for practical jokers and a chance to wear funny hats. It dates back to Moorish times. ◈ *28 Dec*

Left **SeaLife** Right **Mini Hollywood**

⑩ Children's Attractions

1 Muelle de las Carabelas, La Rábida, Huelva Province

Down by the waterfront, the "Pier of the Caravels" is a great treat for kids. They'll love the chance to climb aboard full-size replicas of Columbus's ships *Niña*, *Pinta* and *Santa María* and imagine themselves setting sail to discover the New World. There's also a recreation of a 15th-century European village *(see p89)*. ❧ *Paraje de La Rábida • Map A4 • Open 10am–2pm, 5–9pm Tue–Fri, 11am–8pm Sat–Sun (summer); 10am–7pm Tue–Sun (winter) • 959 53 05 97 • Adm*

2 Parque Zoológico, Jerez

Primarily, this is a care station for the rehabilitation of injured animals, in particular indigenous endangered species. As a result, it can give children a close-up encounter with the wonderful Iberian lynx, which is extremely rare in the wild. There are also white tigers, red pandas and ibis *(see p46)*.

3 Isla Mágica, Seville

This amusement park occupies part of what was Expo '92. One of its themes is to recreate the exploits of the explorers who set out from Seville on voyages of discovery in the 16th century – rides have names such as Jaguar, Anaconda and Orinoco. There are also boat tours and a range of shows. ❧ *Pabellón España, Isla de Cartuja • Map J1 • Hours vary, call ahead for opening times • 902 16 17 16 • www.islamagica.es • Adm*

4 Carromato de Max, Mijas

Claiming to be a compendium of the world's smallest curiosities, this is certainly an oddball collection. There's a fine copy of Da Vinci's *The Last Supper*, executed on a grain of rice, fleas in full suits of clothing and a bust of Churchill's head sculpted from a stick of chalk. ❧ *Avda del Compás • Map D5 • Open 10am–10pm daily (summer); 9am–7pm daily (winter) • 952 58 90 34 • Adm*

5 Tívoli World, Benalmádena

Attractions at this theme park include a flamenco extravaganza and a Wild West show, but Tívoli World is really all about rides. None of them will particularly appeal to adrenaline addicts, but what it lacks in speed it makes up for in old-fashioned fun. ❧ *Avda de Tívoli • Map D5 • Opening times vary monthly; check the website for more details • 952 57 70 16 • www.tivoli.es • Adm*

Tívoli World

For tips on travelling with children in Andalucía See p135

6 SeaLife, Benalmádena

Viewing rescued sharks, seahorses, seals, turtles and other sea creatures is a wonderful experience for kids. They will also love the Lost City of Atlantis, the Mediterranean Tunnel and the Touchpool. ◈ *Puerto Deportivo de Benalmádena • Map D5 • Open Oct–Mar: 10am–6pm daily; Apr–Jun & Sep: 10am–8pm; Jul & Aug: 10am–midnight • 952 56 01 50 • www.sealifeeurope.com • Adm*

7 Cuevas de Nerja

Only discovered in 1959, these caves go back some five million years. The chambers will stimulate children's imagination – with a little help from fanciful names and evocative lighting. The central column in Cataclysm Hall is the tallest in the world, the product of waterdrops falling over countless aeons. ◈ *Ctra Maro • Map E5 • Open 10am–2pm, 4–6:30pm daily (Jul–Aug: to 8pm) • 952 52 95 20 • Adm*

8 Aqua Tropic, Almuñécar

Hours of fun with rides called Kamikazee, Wavebreaker, Ring Rapids, Blackhole Rapids, Soft Runs and a special Children's Lake for the littlest ones. ◈ *Playa de Velilla • Map F5 • Open Jun–Sep: 11am–7pm daily • 958 63 20 81 • Adm*

Cuevas de Nerja

9 Mini Hollywood, Almería

The Wild West rides again at this old "spaghetti western" movie set. At show time the kids can see Jesse James reach his ignominious end *(see p111)*.

10 Parque Acuático Vera, Vera

This place will save the day when what your children need most is to cool off. Five pools of various sizes, loads of undulating slides and tubes, as well as shaded areas. ◈ *Ctra Vera/Garrucha-Villaricos • Map H4 • Open mid-May–Jun & Sep: 11am–6pm daily, Jul & Aug: 11am–7:30pm daily • 950 46 73 37 • www.aquavera.com • Adm*

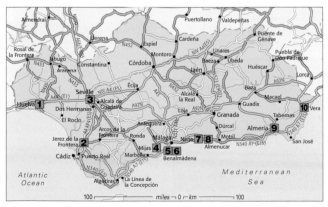

Left **Taracea craftsman from Granada** Right **Ceramic dishes**

Andalucían Souvenirs

1 Granada Pottery
Andalucía's most famous pottery celebrates the symbol of Granada, the pomegranate, and is glazed in turquoise and cobalt blue over white.

2 Granada Taracea
Granada's Moorish-inspired marquetry uses bone, mother-of-pearl, amber and marble in the finest inlays, although humbler objects employ coloured wood chips. You'll find chessboards, tables and boxes of all sizes.

3 Moroccan Crafts
The Albaicín area of Granada *(see pp12–13)* has become a mini-Morocco. Here you can buy leather slippers, embroidered robes, silver tea services and decorative ceramics.

4 Flamenco and Traditional Accessories
If you plan on attending a *romería (see p60)* or any other local festival – or you just feel like taking home a bit of local colour – consider investing in some traditional flamenco paraphernalia. Embroidered silk shawls, ornate tortoiseshell combs and hand-painted silk and ivory fans are the top of the line, but there are plenty of more affordable versions. Synthetic shawls, these days often imported from China, wood or even plastic combs and paper and wood fans are all just as vivid.

5 Silver and Gold Filigree
Two cities, Córdoba and Granada, are known for their delicate filigree work in precious metals. Since ancient times, when Andalucían mines were a primary source of silver and gold for the Mediterranean, craftsmen have created brooches, earrings and necklaces. Designs often reflect the Moorish taste for complex geometrics, but can also depict insects, birds or lizards, set with precious stones.

6 Woodwork
Furniture manufacture of high-quality mahogany items takes place in Cádiz Province, while Ronda is known for its rustic styles and Granada Province is reputed for Mudéjar *(Capiliera)* and Renaissance *(Baza)* styles. Also of note, of course, are Andalucían guitars, with excellent examples created in Algodonales (Cádiz Province) and Marmolejo (Jaén Province), as well as in the main centres of Granada, Córdoba and Seville.

Traditional Spanish fans

When shopping in markets for traditional crafts, the ancient art of haggling is acceptable, even expected.

7 Iron and Metalwork

Wrought-iron and other metal pieces that might tempt you include tin lamps from Úbeda, grilles from Arcos de la Frontera and Torredonjimeno, cowbells from Cortegana and locks from Estepona and Cártama.

8 Leather

Leather goods of all sorts abound. Principal towns of production include Jerez de la Frontera, Almodóvar del Río, Almonte and Ubrique for bags, belts, gloves and jackets. For handmade shoes try Montoro; for handmade boots, Valverde del Camino, both in Huelva Province.

Most traditional are *cordovans* – embossed and hand-decorated leather pieces from Córdoba.

Leather bag

9 Ceramics

Ceramics come in almost as many styles and forms as there are towns – items as diverse as traditional *azulejos* (glazed tiles), *botijos* (double-spouted pitchers) and Hispano-Moorish lustreware. Most tend towards the Islamic style but many carry on the European tradition of depicting scenes from daily life or myths.

10 Weavings

The various weaving arts are well represented in Andalucía. Wickerwork and basketry are notable in Almería, Níjar, Jerez, Lanjarón and Jaén. *Jarapas* (handwoven rugs and blankets) are famous in Almería Province, as well as in Arcos de la Frontera, Grazalema in Cádiz Province, and Las Alpujarras in Jaén Province.

Top 10 Local Produce

1 Fish and Seafood

Mediterranean and Atlantic bounty offers a vast array of fish and shellfish.

2 Olives

Introduced in ancient times, the olive and its oil are vital to Andalucían cuisine. Try olives stuffed with anchovies, or cured with spices and herbs.

3 Grapes

Also dating from ancient times, cultivation of the vine remains a vital part of life.

4 Garlic and Spices

Ajo (garlic) plays a large part in Andalucían cooking, while spices introduced by the Moors include cumin, cinnamon, coriander and saffron.

5 Ham

The most noteworthy hams are from Jabugo and Trevélez.

6 Almonds and Fruits

Almonds are used mainly in honey-based desserts. Fresh fruits include *chirimoyas* (custard apples), figs, pomegranates and persimmons.

7 Meats

The taste for *cordero* (lamb) and *cabra* (goat) can be traced back to the Moorish/Jewish period. *Rabo de toro* (oxtail) is a popular dish.

8 Game

In mountainous areas, rabbit, hare, wild boar, quail, pigeon, pheasant, partridge and venison appear on menus.

9 Vegetables

Artichokes and asparagus were introduced by the Moors; potatoes and tomatoes came from the New World. Wild mushrooms also grow here.

10 Cheese

Goat's and sometimes sheep's milk are used to make most local cheeses.

Left **Bodegas Gomara** Right **Moorish cellar, Pedro Domecq**

🔟 Bodegas and Wineries

1 Pedro Domecq

One of the most legendary of the names associated with sherry, with a flawless discernment for this world-class tipple. The company was founded in 1730, and a tour of the famous Moorish-style cellar "de la Ina" is *de rigueur* when in Jerez *(see p98)*. ◈ *C/San Ildefonso 3, Jerez • Map B5 • 956 15 15 00 • Tours 2pm Tue, Thu & Sat • Adm*

2 González-Byass

Although most of the main sherry producers are now largely owned by British multinationals, this *bodega* is an encouraging example of one that was bought back by the family. Founded in 1835, their operation has two historic cellars, as well as the original tasting room. ◈ *C/Manuel María González 12, Jerez • Map B5 • 902 44 00 77 • www.bodegastiopepe. com • Tours 11am, noon, 1pm, 2pm, 4pm, 5pm & 6pm Mon–Sat; 11am, noon, 1pm & 2pm Sun • Adm*

González-Byass cellar

3 Sandeman

The distinctive silhouetted figure of The Don, in a black cape and wide-brimmed hat, dates from 1928 and is one of the first trademark images ever created. The House of Sandeman was founded in London in 1790; the tour includes tastings. ◈ *C/Pizarro 10, Jerez • Map B5 • 956 31 29 95 • www. sandeman.eu • Tours 11:30am, 12:30pm, 1:30pm Mon, Wed, Fri (also 2:30pm Apr– Oct); 10:30am, noon, 1pm, 2pm Tue, Thu (also 3pm Apr–Oct); Sat by appt • Adm*

4 Osborne Bodega

The black cutout of the noble bull adorning many Andalucían roadside hills is the symbol of this venerable sherry and brandy producer and a protected part of regional heritage. ◈ *C/Los Moros, El Puerto de Santa María • Map B5 • 956 86 91 00 • Tours 10:30am Mon– Fri (call to book); 11am Sat • Adm*

5 Bodegas Alvear, Montilla

What distinguishes the wines here is two-fold. Giant terracotta containers *(tinajas)* are sunk into the ground to keep the contents at a constant temperature, while the hot climate ripens the grapes for a stronger wine *(see p120)*.

6 Bodegas Robles, Montilla

This organic wine producer employs an old system called *solera*, in which young wines on top are blended with older ones below, until they mature. ◈ *Ctra. Córdoba-Málaga km 47 • Map D3 • 957 65 00 63 • Tours by appt*

Bodega *is the Spanish term for a wine cellar.*

7 Bodega El Pimpi, Málaga
Not only can you get the best of Andalucía's vintages here, but there's also a good selection of Spain's finest, such as Ribera del Duero. Delicious *tapas*, too. ◊ C/Granada 68 • Map R5 • 952 22 89 90 • Open daily

8 Bodegas Gomara
This *bodega* produces the traditional Málaga wines as well as its own *fino*, which is dry and pale. They sell the wines in souvenir bottles that may take the form of a matador, a guitar or castanets. ◊ Pol. Campanilla 232, Málaga • Map E5 • 952 43 41 95

Andalucían vintner

9 Bodegas Andrade
This *bodega* was one of the first to realize the potential of the Zalema grape varietal for creating young wines. ◊ Avda Coronación, 35, Bollullos Par del Condado, Huelva • Map A4 • 959 41 01 06

10 Agroalimentaria Virgen del Rocío
This producer has taken use of the Zalema grape a step or two further. A series of large underground fermenting vats form a subterranean cellar, where they make Andalucía's only sparkling wine, Raigal. ◊ Almonte, Huelva • Map B4 • 959 40 61 03 • Tours by appt

Top 10 Sherries and Wines

1 Fino
Clear, crisp and dry, with an aroma of almonds, *fino* is served chilled as an aperitif.

2 Manzanilla
The *fino* sherry made in Sanlúcar de Barrameda. It is dry, pale and slightly salty.

3 Oloroso
The layer of flor yeast is thin, or absent, as a *fino* ages, allowing partial oxidation. *Oloroso* is a rich amber, with an aroma of hazelnuts.

4 Amontillado
Midway between a *fino* and an *oloroso*. The layer of flor yeast is allowed to die off, so it gets darker in colour.

5 Palo Cortado
This has an aroma reminiscent of an *amontillado*, while its colour is closer to *oloroso*.

6 Cream Sherry
This international favourite results when you take an *oloroso* and sweeten it by mixing in a measure of Pedro Ximénez wine.

7 Pedro Ximénez
This naturally sweet wine, when aged with care, is elegant and velvety.

8 Brandy de Jerez
This brandy is made by ageing wine spirits in casks that have previously been used to age sherry. It is sweeter and more caramelized than French brandy.

9 Málaga
Málaga's famous sweet wines are made from the Moscatel and Pedro Ximénez grape varieties.

10 Raigal
The region's only sparkling wine is refreshing on the palate.

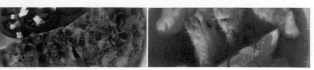

Left **Tortilla española** Right **Fish soup**

Andalucían Dishes

1 Gazpacho

This signature Andalucían dish is a cold soup made of fresh tomatoes, green peppers, cucumber, garlic, olive oil, wine vinegar or lemon, breadcrumbs and salt. There are dozens of local variations of this nourishing refresher, which may involve almonds, grapes, melon, strawberries, red peppers, and boiled egg or chopped ham garnishes.

Gazpacho

2 Tortilla Española and Patatas Bravas

Both of these dishes are ubiquitous not just in Andalucía but all over Spain. The first is a dense potato omelette with onions, fried into a savoury cake. It is served cold by the slice and is so filling it can make a full meal. The second consists of fried potato wedges served with a spicy sauce.

3 Fish Soups

The array of *sopas de mariscos* or *pescado* (shellfish or fish soups) seems to be limited only to the cooks' imagination. Málaga favourites include *sopa viña*, a sherry-spiked version, and *cachoreñas*, with orange flavouring. Cádiz is known for its *guisos marineros* (seafood stews), made with the best fish of the region.

4 Calamares

All along the coast, you will encounter whole baby *calamares* (squids) served grilled – the essence of simplicity and delicious as long as they are fresh. A common alternative is to cut them into rings and batter-fry them – again, if they are fresh, they will taste sweet and tender. A complete *fritura de pescado* or *fritura mixta* (mixed fish fry) might add anchovies, prawns, chunks of cod or whatever is good that day.

Calamares

5 Rape

Monkfish *(rape)*, also called anglerfish, is one of the top choices for quality maritime eating in Andalucía. Only the tail of this very unprepossessing looking fish is eaten, and it has a succulent quality similar to lobster tail or scallops. It is preferably served grilled, but can also be stewed in a rich sauce, most likely to be tomato-based.

6 Arroza a la Marinera

This is the Andalucían version of *paella*, an appellation that also appears on some menus. Saffron-flavoured rice is served with an assortment of fish and shellfish, which can

Vegetarians, and especially vegans, will face very narrow choices – mostly salads – in Andalucían restaurants.

Arroza a la Marinera

include prawns, clams and squid. Unlike the Valencia variety, it does not generally include sausage or chicken. The dish is also known as *arroz con mariscos*.

7 Salads
Andalucían *ensaladas* (salads) are substantial and often come with asparagus, hard-boiled eggs, tuna, artichoke, olives and onions, in addition to lettuce and tomato. You can ask that any of these ingredients be left off your order if you prefer.

8 Valle de los Pedroches
This soft sheep's cheese from Córdoba Province is typical of the regional type: strong in taste. The cheese is preserved in olive oil and enhanced with herbs.

9 Dessert Tarts
The variety of cakes and sweet biscuits you will see typically involve Moorish ingredients such as anise, sesame, almonds and cinnamon. Most are also sweetened with honey rather than sugar. Two common types are *alfajores*, with honey and almonds, and *piononos*, which are soaked in liqueur.

10 Tocino de Cielo
This rich egg custard pudding or flan is made by nuns in Jerez de la Frontera and elsewhere in Cádiz Province.

Top 10 Drinks

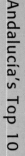

1 Sherry
The region's most famous wine comes from Cádiz Province (see p67).

2 Brandy
Brandy is distilled in Cádiz Province, Córdoba Province and Huelva Province.

3 Wine
Málaga's sweet wines come from Moscatel and Pedro Ximenez grapes, while fruity Condado wines are produced from Zalema grapes.

4 Beer
Cruz Campo is a local, Pilsner-type *cerveza* (beer) that is among Spain's best.

5 Liqueur
Aniseed-based liqueurs come primarily from Montilla in Córdoba Province. Other liqueurs include *aguardiente* from Huelva Province and *cazalla* from Sevilla Province.

6 Sangría
This classic red wine punch is world famous. The lighter *Tinto de Verano* is very popular in Andalucía.

7 Coffee
Opt for *café solo (espresso)* or *cortado* (espresso with very little milk). *Café con leche* (coffee with milk) is drunk for breakfast.

8 Mint Tea
Moroccan-style *teterías* serving mint tea are popping up more and more (see p116).

9 Soft Drinks
Refrescos include *batidos* (milkshakes), *granizados* (iced fruit crush) and *horchata* (a milky drink made from a tuber).

10 Mineral Water
Bottled water, *sin gas* (still) or *con gas* (fizzy), is available, the best being from Lanjarón in Granada Province.

If you want a glass of draft beer, rather than bottled beer, ask for una caña.

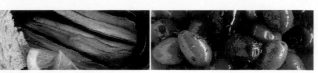

Left **Anchoas** Right **Aceitunas**

TOP10 Tapas Dishes

1 Aceitunas

There are innumerable types of olives, from small to large, green to black, salty to sweet, or whole to stuffed. The name of the dish can be confusing – although the Spanish name for the tree is the *olivo*, which comes from Latin, the word for the fruit comes from the Arabic *az-zait*, which means "juice of the olive".

2 Chorizo al Vino

Chorizos are spicy, paprika-red garlic sausages that can be served grilled, sautéed with wine *(al vino)*, or stewed with other ingredients. They are generally made of pork. *Morcilla* (blood sausage or black pudding) is a classic country delicacy.

3 Jamón Serrano

A complementary slice of ham laid over the top of a *copa* (glass) is said to be how the custom of *tapa* (which literally means "lid") got started. The finest regional type available is mountain-cured ham, but there is also *jamón York* (regular ham), as well as other cured pork products, including a local *tocino* (bacon) and *fiambres* (cold cuts). These are often served with cheese and bread as a perfect complement.

4 Ensaladilla

"Russian salad" is sometimes an option for vegetarians – but not for vegans, as it usually consists of diced vegetables mixed in a thick mayonnaise. Watch out, however, as there are versions with cubes of ham mixed in as well. And make sure that this, and all mayonnaise-based dishes, are freshly prepared.

5 Mariscos

Berberechos (cockles), *almejas* (clams), *mejillones* (mussels), *pulpo* (octopus), *sepia* (cuttlefish) and *zamburiñas* (baby clams) are favourite seafood options everywhere in Spain. Roasted *caracoles* (snails), prepared with garlic, can be a rich but delicious treat.

6 Champiñones al Ajillo

Mushrooms sautéed with garlic are a standard item on *tapas* menus. Other popular vegetable dishes include *judias* (green beans), particularly good stewed with tomatoes and garlic, and *escalibadas* (aubergines/eggplants) served in a salad that also features *pimientos* (green peppers).

Jamón Serrano

Tapas *are usually eaten standing up at the bar; in Granada, they sometimes come free with a drink.*

Anchoas (Boquerones)
7 Anchovies and sardines are often served lightly fried in batter, but can just as likely be offered marinated and preserved in oil, or with a tomato sauce. You generally eat them minus the head but with all the bones.

Croquetas
8 Croquettes are made with chicken or fish and mashed potatoes, formed into balls and deep-fried. A variation on this theme are *soldaditos* (fritters), which can be made of vegetables, chicken or fish.

Albóndigas
9 "Meatballs" can be made from meat or fish and will most likely be stewed in a tomato sauce, together with garlic and spices. An alternative method of preparing chunks of meat, seafood or fish is by skewering them and grilling them as kebabs, either plain or spicy Moroccan-style.

Albóndigas

Alioli
10 This is mayonnaise laced with a powerful dose of garlic and is served as a dish in its own right, for dipping bread into or as a condiment. Another popular relish is *pipirrana*, a compote made of tomato, onion and pepper.

Top 10 Tapas Preparation Styles

Pickled
1 Mixed in with olives, you'll often find miniature gherkins, and possibly pearl onions, bits of garlic and hot peppers.

Marinated
2 Anchovies, sardines and seafood all come marinated. You'll see them sitting out on bars, possibly under glass, steeped in olive oil.

Cured
3 The hams of Andalucía are lightly salted – mountain-cured are the best.

With Mayonnaise
4 Any dish can be an excuse to slather on the *alioli*. Two dishes that often have mayonnaise are *patatas alioli* and *ensaladilla*.

On Bread
5 Many *tapas* don't really come to life until applied to bread. Some are served already perched on a slice.

Egg-Based
6 Eggs are essential in *tortilla (see p68)* or come hard-boiled as a garnish.

Fried
7 Almost anything you can think of will turn up *frito* (batter-fried or sautéed), from fish to mushrooms.

Grilled or Roasted
8 If you want to ingest a little less oil, *a la plancha* (grilled) and *asado* (roasted) are the options to choose.

Stewed
9 *Estofado* variations include fish, meat, potato and vegetables, often in tomato sauce.

A la Marinera
10 This technique, commonly used for fish and seafood, is similar to poaching and involves wine, garlic and parsley.

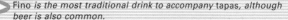

Fino is the most traditional drink to accompany tapas, although beer is also common.

AROUND ANDALUCÍA

ANDALUCÍA'S TOP 10

Left **Courtyard, Museo de Bellas Artes** Right **Tiled sign, Fábrica Real de Tabacos**

Seville

ANDALUCÍA'S CAPITAL IS AN ARISTOCRATIC YET RELAXED CITY, *with a fabulous and ancient cultural heritage that dates back beyond recorded history. Its fate has always been tied to its river, the Río Guadalquivir ("the great river" in Arabic), and the trade it offered the city. Today much of the riverfront is made up of an attractive tree-lined promenade. To take in all of the historic centre of Seville would require at least a week, as there is so much to see in the way of art and architecture as well as distinctive neighbourhoods each with their own charm. But its highlights, including the spectacular cathedral, Moorish and Renaissance palaces and fine museums, are all within walking distance of each other and could be handled in a weekend, giving you just a taste of one of Spain's most beautiful cities.*

Seville Cathedral

🔟 Sights

1. Seville Cathedral & La Giralda
2. Real Alcázar
3. Casa de Pilatos
4. Museo de Bellas Artes
5. Fábrica Real de Tabacos
6. Ayuntamiento
7. Plaza de España
8. Museo Arqueológico
9. Torre del Oro & Torre de Plata
10. Cartuja de Santa María de las Cuevas

Around Andalucía – Seville

600 — yards ¬ 0 — metres ¬ 600

1 Seville Cathedral & La Giralda

Legend has it that when the *sevillanos* decided to build their cathedral in the 15th century, they proclaimed their intention to erect an edifice so huge that later generations would call them mad. They achieved their aim with the largest church (by volume, not floorplan) in Christendom *(see pp14–15)*.

2 Real Alcázar

This exotic palace was primarily the brainchild of Pedro I, who had it built as a lavish love-nest for himself and his mistress, María de Padilla *(see pp16–17)*.

3 Casa de Pilatos

Erroneously said to be based on the house of Pontius Pilate in Jerusalem, this 15th-century gem is the most sumptuous of Seville's urban mansions. It is a delightful blend of Mudéjar (Christian-Islamic), Gothic and Renaissance styles, punctuated with Classical statuary. Look for the head of the Greek boy, Antinous, who died as a teenager and was deified by his grief-stricken lover, Emperor Hadrian, in the 2nd century *(see p38)*. 🖎 *Plaza de Pilatos 1 • Map N3 • 954 22 52 98 • Open 9am–6pm daily • Adm (free Tue for EU members)*

Courtyard, Casa de Pilatos

Domed ceiling, Museo de Bellas Artes

4 Museo de Bellas Artes

Among Spain's finest art repositories, it is second only to the Prado in Madrid for its range of great Spanish paintings. Housed in a former 17th-century convent, the collection focuses on the Seville School, led by Zurbarán, Cano, Murillo and Valdés Leal, including Murillo's touching *Virgen de la Servilleta*. Don't miss El Greco's poignant portrait of his son and the polychrome terracotta of St Jerome by Florentine sculptor Pietro Torregiano, a colleague of Michelangelo's *(see p54)*. 🖎 *Plaza del Museo 9 • Map K2 • 954 78 65 00 • Open 9am–8:30pm Tue–Sat, 9am–2:30pm Sun • Adm (free for EU members)*

5 Fábrica Real de Tabacos

Now a part of Seville University, this handsome 18th-century edifice is the second-largest building in Spain, after El Escorial in Madrid. Famous for its fun-loving female workers, who at one time rolled three-quarters of Europe's cigars, the old factory has been immortalized by *Carmen*, the world's most popular opera. The doomed heroine, a hot-blooded gypsy *cigarrera*, remains, for many, the incarnation of Spanish passion. 🖎 *C/San Fernando 4 • Map M5 • Open 8am–8:30pm Mon–Fri • Free*

Ayuntamiento

This building has been the town hall since the 16th century. Inside, the rooms are decorated with historic paraphernalia of the city and the monarchy, in a blend of Gothic and Renaissance styles. Outside, the façades reflect the evolution of taste, from the original Renaissance Plateresque work with its finely carved stonework, to the 19th-century attempt to copy the style, seen from Plaza de San Francisco (*see p38*). ✎ *Plaza Nueva 1 • Map L3 • 954 59 01 45 • Open for pre-booked guided tours only, mid-Sep–Jul: 5:30 & 6pm Tue–Thu, noon Sat • Free*

Plaza de España

This semicircular plaza was designed as the centrepiece for the Ibero-American Exposition of 1929. Almost completely covered with gorgeous glazed tiles, its surfaces depict historic moments and heraldic symbols of the 40 regions of Spain. A boating canal follows the arc of the structure, crossed by colourful footbridges. The site was used as a set in the film *Star Wars: Attack of the Clones*, for its other-worldly feel. ✎ *Map N6*

Feria de Abril

The six-day Spring Fair, about two weeks after Easter, is a riot of colour and high spirits. Andalucían horses strut on parade, ridden by *caballeros* in traditional leather chaps, waistcoats and wide-brimmed *sombreros cordobeses*, often with dazzling, flower-like women perched behind. The air is alive with music, the fairgrounds overflow with *casetas* (party marquees – most of them by invitation only), and drinking and dancing continue until dawn. All the Feria festivities take place south of the river.

Museo Arqueológico

Museo Arqueológico

This Renaissance-style pavilion was also one of the fabulous structures created for the 1929 Exposition and now houses Andalucía's principal archaeological museum. The assemblage of artifacts ranges from Paleolithic finds, exhibited in the basement, to splendours of Roman and Moorish art, displayed on the upper floors. Outstanding are the Carambolo treasures of Tartessian gold, and the Roman sculpture collection is Spain's most prestigious. ✎ *Parque María Luisa • 954 78 64 74 • Open 9am–8:30pm Tue–Sat, 9am–2:30pm Sun • Adm*

Torre del Oro & Torre de Plata

Tradition states that the imposing 13th-century Moorish dodeca-hedral (12-sided) watchtower, the Torre del Oro (Tower of Gold), is named after the golden tiles that once adorned it. Others say its name derives from its use as a warehouse for the gold coming in from the New World during Seville's heyday. It now houses a small maritime museum. Nearby stands the Torre de Plata (Tower of Silver), a more modest octagonal tower, which most likely gets its name as a complement to its neighbour. Both towers originally formed part of the city's defences. ◊ *Torre del Oro: Paseo de Colón; Map L4; Open Sep–Jul: 10am–2pm Tue–Fri, 11am–2pm Sat–Sun; Adm (except Tue)* • *Torre de Plata: C/Santander; Map L4; 954 22 24 19; Closed to the public*

🔟 Cartuja de Santa María de las Cuevas

This 15th-century monastery has had its ups and downs over the centuries. During Spain's Golden Age it was the favoured retreat of Christopher Columbus, whose remains were interred here for several decades. The monks went on to decorate their vast enclave with commissions from some of Seville's greatest artists – most of the works are now in the Museo de Bellas Artes *(see p75)*. In 1841 it became a ceramics factory. Finally restored as part of Expo '92, the complex is today home to a contemporary art museum. ◊ *Isla de Cartuja* • *Map J1* • *Centro Andaluz de Arte Contemporáneo: 955 03 70 70; www. caac.es; Open 10am–8pm Tue–Fri (Apr–Sep: to 9pm), 11am–8pm Sat (Apr–Sep: to 9pm), 10am–3pm Sun; Adm (free Tue)*

Torre del Oro

A Half-Day Walk Around the Barrio de Santa Cruz

🕐 Start at the exit to the **Real Alcázar** *(see pp16–17)*, which is on Patio de las Banderas. Turn right to find the Arco de la Judería, a covered alleyway that leads to the Callejón del Agua, running along the old Jewish Quarter's southern wall. As you proceed, you will be able to peep into some of the famously lush patios of these perfectly whitewashed houses. The writer Washington Irving once stayed at No. 2. After the wall ends, you'll see the **Jardines de Murillo** on your right *(see p79)*, where you can enjoy a tranquil stroll.

Then turn back to find **Plaza Santa Cruz** *(see p79)*, where the church that gave the neighbourhood its name once stood, until it was burned down by the French in 1810. A 17th-century wrought-iron cross stands here now. Cross a couple of streets west to find the **Hospital de los Venerables** *(see p78)*, and take in its delightful central courtyard and important art gallery. From here, go east to Calle Santa Teresa 8, the former home of the great artist Bartolomé Murillo *(see p56)*, who died here in 1682 after a fall while painting frescoes in Cádiz.

Finally, work your way back towards the **Cathedral** *(see pp14–15)* along Calle Mesón del Moro and then to Calle Mateos Gago. At No. 1 you'll find the Cervecería Giralda *(954 22 74 35)*, excellent for a drink and some *tapas* for either lunch or dinner.

Left **La Maestranza bullring** Right **Detail, Hospital de los Venerables**

Best of the Rest

1 Archivo de Indias
Established in 1785, this is a storehouse for documents relating to the Spanish colonization of the New World *(see p54)*. ◈ *Avda de la Constitución 3 • Map M4 • Open 8am–3pm Mon–Fri • 954 50 05 28 • Free*

2 Hospital de los Venerables
Founded in the 17th century as a home for the elderly, this is now a cultural centre. The church features a *trompe-l'oeil* ceiling by Juan de Valdés Leal. ◈ *Plaza de Doña Elvira 8 • Map M4 • Open 10am–2pm, 4–8pm daily • 954 56 26 96 • Adm*

3 Museo de Artes y Costumbres Populares
Exhibits here include displays on flamenco and bullfighting. ◈ *Plaza de América 3 • Open 2:30–8:30pm Tue, 9am–8:30pm Wed–Sat, 9am–2:30pm Sun • 954 71 23 91 • Adm*

4 Hospital de la Caridad
This hospital was founded by reformed rake Miguel de Mañara, the inspiration for the mythical Don Juan. ◈ *C/Temprado 3 • Map L4 • Open 9am–1:30pm, 3:30–6:30pm Mon–Sat, 9am–1pm Sun • 954 22 32 32 • Adm*

5 La Maestranza
The "Cathedral of Bullfighting" becomes the focal point when the sporting season opens in April. ◈ *Paseo de Colón 12 • Map L3 • Open daily • 954 21 03 15*

6 Barrio de Triana
This quarter, once home to Seville's gypsies, was known for producing flamenco artists and bullfighters. It still creates fine ceramics *(see p82)*. ◈ *Map K4*

7 Casa de la Condesa de Lebrija
A 15th-century mansion, embellished with mosaics from Itálica *(see p89)*. ◈ *C/Cuna 8 • Map M2 • Open Mon–Sat • 954 21 81 83 • Adm*

8 Camara Oscura
This huge camera obscura displays a moving image of the area around the Torre de los Perdigones. ◈ *C/Resolana • Map M1 • Open daily • 902 10 10 81 • Adm*

9 La Macarena
This district is home to the Iglesia de San Luis, a sumptuous Rococo church; the 15th-century Convento de Santa Paula; and Seville's adored religious icon, the Virgen de la Macarena. During Semana Santa *(see p60)* she is paraded on a silver float. ◈ *Map N1*

10 Museo del Baile Flamenco
This museum will help unlock the magical world of flamenco. ◈ *C/ Manuel Rojas Marcos 3 • Map M3 • Open daily • 954 34 03 11 • Adm*

On the way out of the Convento de Santa Paula you can acquire some of the nuns' famous marmalades and other delights.

Left **Parque María Luísa** Right **Columbus monument, Jardines de Murillo**

🔟 Parks, Paseos and Plazas

1 Real Alcázar
These gardens are a blend of Moorish and Italian Renaissance styles *(see pp16–17)*.

2 Parque de María Luísa
This park dominates the southern end of the city. Its present design, comprising the immense Plaza de España, was laid out for the 1929 Exposition. Look for peacocks in the trees. Beware of pickpockets. ✎ *Map M6*

3 Plaza de San Francisco and Plaza Nueva
These squares represent the heart of the city. Plaza de San Francisco (also called Plaza Mayor) is Seville's oldest and the focal point of public spectacles. Plaza Nueva is a pleasant park with a monument to King Fernando the Saint. ✎ *Map L3 & M3*

4 Jardines de Murillo
These formal gardens used to be the orchards and vegetable plots for the Alcázar. Donated to the city in 1911, they are named after Seville painter Bartolomé Murillo *(see p56)*. A monument to Columbus features the bronze prows of the *Santa María*, the caravel that bore him to the New World in 1492. ✎ *Map N4*

5 Plaza de Santa Cruz
Created when Napoleon's soldiers destroyed a church that once stood here, this square is now adorned by an iron cross, La Cruz de la Cerrajería. ✎ *Map N4*

6 Calle Sierpes
This pedestrianized promenade is the principal shopping street of old Seville. It's also the place to be seen during the early evening *paseo*. ✎ *Map L2*

7 Alameda de Hércules
Set off by pairs of columns at either end – the southern set are ancient Roman and are surmounted by 16th-century sculptures of Hercules and Julius Caesar – this promenade has been renovated and lined with trendy bars and restaurants, which draw a bohemian crowd. ✎ *Map M1*

8 Plaza de la Alfalfa
Once the location of the hay market, and later home to a Sunday morning pet market, the Alfalfa is now a good area for browsing. Visit clothing stores, including several flamenco boutiques and unique accessory shops, or sit in its bars and restaurants. ✎ *Map M2*

9 Paseo Alcalde Marqués de Contadero
With the Torre del Oro at one end *(see p77)*, this tree-lined riverfront promenade makes for a pleasant stroll. ✎ *Map L4*

10 Calle San Fernando and Avenida de la Constitución
These two streets create a pedestrian promenade through the heart of Seville. Strolls here are livened up by monthly art and photo exhibitions. ✎ *Map M5*

Following pages: **Parque María Luisa**

Left **El Mercadillo** Right **El Corte Inglés sign**

Shops and Markets

1 El Corte Inglés
Although you're unlikely to find any bargains here, the range of merchandise is impressive. Spain's main department store chain carries not only clothes and accessories, but also perfume, housewares, decorative items, CDs and sporting goods. There's also a food hall and supermarket, which stock gourmet foods. ◈ *Plaza del Duque de la Victoria 8 • Map L2*

2 Mango
For the latest in younger women's fashion trends, this is the place to come. ◈ *C/Velazquez 7–9 • Map L2*

3 Zara
Here you'll find hip, affordable clothing for the entire family. In summer, the linen blends and light cottons are just right for the Andalucían climate. Scents and sunglasses too. ◈ *Plaza del Duque de la Victoria • Map L2*

4 Angeles Méndez
This is a good spot to load up on all the flouncy dresses, mantillas, shawls and so forth that you will need to participate in the various festivals that abound in the region *(see pp60–61)*. ◈ *C/Alcaicería de la Loza 24 • Map M2*

5 Compás Sur
For music lovers there are CDs, DVDs and books covering a variety of genres from Fúsion to Flamenco. ◈ *C/Cuesta del Rosario 7-E; 954 21 56 62 • Map M2*

6 Sargadelos
Household items with an artful twist are the speciality here. Complete dinner and tea or coffee services are traditional but at the same time inventive. ◈ *C/Albareda 17; 954 21 67 08 • Map L3*

7 El Mercadillo
Just off the Alameda de Hércules *(see p79)*, El Jueves flea market, held every Thursday, consists mostly of old junk, books and posters. Still, it's fun to look for the occasional treasure. But beware of pickpockets. ◈ *C/de la Feria • Map M1*

8 Hippy Market
This is the place to find handmade jewellery, leather goods and cheap clothes. Thursday to Saturday. ◈ *Plaza del Duque de la Victoria • Map L2*

9 Old Train Station Shopping Centre
The old Córdoba train station has been restored to its former beauty and is now home to a shopping centre and entertainment complex. ◈ *Antigua Estación de Córdoba, Plaza de Armas • Map K2*

10 Cerámica Santa Ana
The place to buy the famous Triana pottery. In operation since 1870, this shop sells everything from replicas of 16th-century tiles to ashtrays. Similar workshops can be found on Calle Covadonga. ◈ *C/San Jorge 31, Barrio de Triana; 954 33 81 76 • Map K4*

For more on Andalucían souvenirs **See pp64–5**

Left **Teatro de la Maestranza** Right **Teatro Lope de Vega**

🔟 Flamenco and Theatre Venues

1 Teatro de la Maestranza
Seville's main theatre was built on a former munitions works, as part of Expo '92. It serves primarily as the city's opera house, putting on productions of all the standards, particularly those set in Seville, including *Carmen*, *Don Juan*, *The Marriage of Figaro* and *The Barber of Seville*. ✆ *Paseo de Colón 22; 954 22 33 44 • www.teatrode lamaestranza.com • Map L4*

2 Teatro Lope de Vega
Named after the "Spanish Shakespeare", this neo-Baroque theatre was built in 1929 as a casino and theatre for the Ibero-American Exposition. Modern and classical works, both musical and dramatic, are performed here. ✆ *Avda de María Luisa; 954 59 08 67 • www.teatrolopedevega.org • Map M5 • Closed Jul–Aug*

3 Teatro Alameda
Popular performances of all genres take to the stage of this modest theatre, with a strong emphasis on flamenco. It's also a good venue for contemporary Andalucían theatrical works. ✆ *C/Crédito 11; 954 90 01 64*

4 Teatro Central
In season, this theatre highlights the *Flamenco Viene del Sur* series, concurrently with all sorts of theatre, dance and classical music. It's a starkly modern facility right on the river. ✆ *C/José de Gálvez, Isla de Cartuja; 955 03 72 00 • Map J1 • Closed Jul–Sep*

5 Centro Cultural Cajasol
This venue hosts concerts, art exhibitions, films and other performances. ✆ *C/Laraña 4; 901 21 48 48 • Map M2*

6 El Arenal
The least tacky of the flamenco shows aimed at tourists, although without the soul-stirring authenticity of the real thing. If you come for the first show, the second is free. *(See p59)*.

7 La Carbonería
A relaxed and authentic bar. Flamenco shows tend to happen on Monday and Thursday nights. ✆ *C/Levies 18; 954 21 44 60 • Map N3*

8 Los Gallos
Despite its popularity with tourists, the atmosphere here is genuine. First-rate flamenco performers. ✆ *Plaza de Santa Cruz 11; 954 21 69 81 • www.tablaolosgallos.com • Map N4 • Shows 9pm & 11:30pm daily*

9 Casa de la Memoria de al-Andalus
This cultural centre is dedicated to Jewish influence. Top flamenco artists and renditions of Sephardic music. ✆ *C/Ximénes de Enciso 28; 954 56 06 70 • Map N3 • Shows 9pm daily*

10 El Patio Sevillano
Another venue that caters to the throngs of tourists who want a rousing flamenco show. ✆ *Paseo de Cristobal Colón 11A; 954 21 41 20 • www.elpatiosevillano.com • Map L4 • Shows 7:30pm & 10pm daily*

Left **Sala Malandar** Right **El Riconcillo**

Tapas Bars & Nightlife

Sala Malandar
Come to this relaxed club for an eclectic array of music – from funk and rare groove to reggae and ska via soul, folk and indie pop – supplied by either live bands or DJs. ◈ *C/Torneo 43 • Map K1 • 954 37 50 12 • No credit cards*

Naima Café
Small but rich in atmosphere, this jazz bar has a relaxed, unpretentious feel. Jazz memorabilia adorns the wall, and there is live music at the weekend. ◈ *C/Trajano 45 • Map L1 • No credit cards*

Casa Morales
Reputedly the second-oldest bar in town (1850), and it doesn't seem to have changed much. Drinks are still poured from old casks. Simple *tapas*. ◈ *C/García de Vinuesa 11 • Map L3 • 954 22 12 42*

Antigüedades
The interior decor of this bar changes every few months, but it is always delightfully eccentric, with masks, bizarre dolls or giant tarantulas. The reasonably priced beers make it popular with locals and tourists alike. ◈ *C/Argote de Molina 40 • Map M3 • No credit cards*

Bar San Lorenzo
Virtually the same since it opened in 1893; expect a littered floor, old wood, lots of regulars and some choice comestibles. An Alameda district institution. ◈ *Plaza de San Lorenzo 7 • Map L1 • 954 38 15 58 • No credit cards*

El Rinconcillo
The city's oldest *taberna* dates from 1670 and is an essential stop on your Seville itinerary. Said to be the place where *tapa* was invented. ◈ *C/Gerona 40 • Map M2 • 954 22 31 83*

Antique
Dress to impress at Seville's most upscale club, and you might just get past the doormen. In summer, the outdoor terrace Aqua hosts live performances of all types. Be ready to party until sunrise. ◈ *C/Matemáticos Rey Pastor y Castro, La Cartuja • 954 46 22 07*

Santo Terraza
This is the place to see and be seen. Enjoy the spectacular views of the cathedral and the Giralda while sipping on a cocktail. Reservations recommended. ◈ *C/Alemanes 27, 4th Floor of EME fusionhotel • Map M3 • 954 56 00 00 • Closed in winter*

El Garlochi
An institution in Seville, El Garlochi is one of the city's most unusual bars thanks to its religious decor. Expect Baroque exuberance and lively locals. ◈ *C/Boteros 26 • Map M2 • 663 62 39 04*

Bar Bistec
The "Steak Bar" is another characteristic Triana venue, traditional and full of local colour. It stays open late, as does almost everything in Andalucía. ◈ *C/Pelay Correa 34 • Map K4 • 954 27 47 59*

Note that many Spanish bars and restaurants do not open until about 9pm for their evening trade.

Price Categories

For a three-course	**€** under €20
meal for one with half	**€€** €20–€30
a bottle of wine (or	**€€€** €30–€40
equivalent meal), taxes	**€€€€** €40–€50
and extra charges.	**€€€€€** over €50

Above **Abades Triana**

TOP 10 More Places to Eat

1 Torre de los Perdigones
Traditional Spanish cuisine with a twist. Try the *margret de pato con salsa de miel y limon* (duck breast with honey and lemon sauce). ✆ *C/Resolana • Map L1 • 954 90 93 53 • DA • €€€*

2 ConTenedor
Located in the bohemian neighbourhood of Macarena, this local café is popular with creative types who enjoy a new take on traditional flavours. ✆ *San Luis 50 • Map N1 • 954 91 63 33 • €€*

3 La Alicantina
Enjoy seafood delicacies as you watch the hubbub on this busy square. ✆ *Plaza del Salvador 2–3 • Map M3 • 954 22 61 22 • €€€*

4 La Albahaca
Set in a converted mansion, decorated with *azulejo* tiles. The seasonal menu may feature fish, wild mushrooms or almonds. ✆ *Plaza Santa Cruz 12 • Map N4 • 954 22 07 14 • €€€*

5 Hostería del Laurel
Mentioned in the 19th-century play *Don Juan*, this Santa Cruz favourite has hams hanging from the ceiling. The *tapas* are as memorable as the ambience. ✆ *Plaza de los Venerables 5 • Map M4 • 954 22 02 95 • €€€*

6 Casa Plácido
Convenient for all the major sights, this venerable bar has hams dangling, barrels of sherry, old posters and traditional *tapas*. ✆ *C/Mesón del Moro 5 & C/Ximenes de Enciso 11 • Map M3 • 954 56 39 71 • €€€*

7 Taberna del Alabardero
This restaurant has earned itself a Michelin star. The setting is sumptuous, while the menu excels in meat dishes and local seafood. ✆ *C/Zaraqoza 20 • Map L3 • 954 50 27 21 • €€€€*

8 Abades Triana
This modern restaurant has a commanding location on the river. Diners can book a spot in *El Cubo*, a private area with a "floating" glass floor. Renowned chef Willy Moya presides over the kitchen. ✆ *C/Betis 69 • Map L5 • 954 28 64 59 • DA • €€€€*

9 Eslava
This *tapas* bar offers specialities such as lamb with honey and courgette (zucchini) quiche. ✆ *C/Eslava 3–5 • Map L1 • 954 90 65 68 • €€*

10 El Faro de Triana
On the Triana side of Seville's oldest bridge, this place has superb views, as well as simple, traditional food. ✆ *Puente de Isabel II • Map K4 • 954 33 61 92 • DA • €€*

Note: Unless otherwise stated, all restaurants accept credit cards and serve some vegetarian dishes such as salad or a tapa

Left **El Rocío** Right **Palace wall painting, Écija**

Sevilla and Huelva Provinces

LEAVING BEHIND THE MAGNETIC ALLURE OF GLORIOUS SEVILLE, *the rest of Sevilla Province and neighbouring Huelva Province are among the least visited areas of Andalucía. Consequently, much of the zone has remained a rural hinterland, where time moves slowly and the old customs prevail. Some of the finest nature preserves are here, too, including the ecologically essential Coto de Doñana, mountainous reaches and pristine beaches, generally frequented by Spaniards rather than tourists. Culturally rich as well, each town and village shelters surprising art treasures and ancient marvels, where you may find yourself the only visitor – a welcome relief after the throngs encountered elsewhere in Andalucía.*

TOP 10 Sights

1. Parque Nacional Coto de Doñana
2. El Rocío
3. Huelva City
4. El Parque Minero de Río Tinto
5. Gruta de las Maravillas
6. Cazalla de la Sierra
7. Écija
8. Osuna
9. Carmona
10. Itálica

Necropolis, Carmona

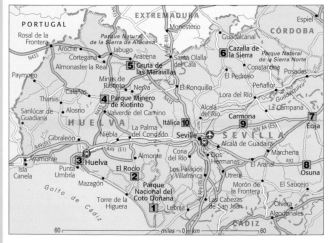

Sign up for DK's email newsletter on traveldk.com

Wetlands, Parque Nacional Coto de Doñana

Parque Nacional Coto de Doñana

Europe's largest nature reserve includes important wetlands and shifting dunes that are gradually moving inland. The fragile ecosystem can only be visited on guided tours *(see pp30–31)*.

El Rocío

The fact that this town resembles an Old West frontier outpost is no accident. The Spaniards who settled what are now the states of Texas, New Mexico and Arizona mostly came from this part of Spain and took their architectural style with them. Horses are still a normal way to get around here – hence the hitching posts. The place bursts into life during the annual Romería, one of Spain's largest festivals *(see p31)*. ◈ *Map B4*

Huelva City

Founded by the Phoenicians, Huelva was at its peak under the Romans – the Museo Provincial holds remarkable archaeological finds. The city's other claim to fame is as the starting point of Columbus's epic voyage *(see p34)*. Huelva was the first port for New World trade, until Seville took over. ◈ *Map A4 • Museo Provincial: Alameda Sundheim 13, 959 65 04 24; Open 2:30–8:30pm Tue, 9am–8pm Wed–Sat, 9am–2:30pm Sun; Adm (free to EU members)*

El Parque Minero de Río Tinto

The Río Tinto (Red River) Mines, the world's oldest, have been exploited as a source of mineral wealth for some 5,000 years, and the gradual stripping away of the rich ore has left a weird moonscape shot through with coloured fissures. A museum details the mines' history. ◈ *Map B3 • Museo Minero: Plaza Ernest Lluch, 959 59 00 25; Open 10:30am–3pm, 4–7pm daily; Adm*

Gruta de las Maravillas

A guided tour of these marvellous caves – Spain's largest – will wind through beautiful chambers with naturally coloured formations and names such as the Hut, Organ, Cathedral, Quail and Twins. The last room is a notorious crowd-pleaser – the *Sala de los Culos* (Chamber of the Buttocks). In addition to the twelve caverns, there are also six underground lakes, which create stunning visual effects. The "Great Lake" lies under a 70 m (230 ft) high vaulted ceiling. ◈ *Map B3 • Pozo de la Nieve, Aracena • 959 12 83 55 • Open 10am–1:30pm, 3–6pm daily • Adm*

Gruta de las Maravillas

It is best to visit the Gruta de las Maravillas in the morning as entrance tickets tend to sell out quickly.

Cazalla de la Sierra

6 The main town in the Sierra Norte is a steep cluster of whitewashed houses. It's a popular place for weekend getaways by *sevillanos* and particularly known for producing some of the area's famous anise-based tipples. Just 3 km (2 miles) outside of town is a former Carthusian monastery, restored as part hotel, part arts centre with gallery. ◈ *Map C3 • La Cartuja de Cazalla arts centre: 954 88 45 16; Open daily; Adm*

Écija

7 Two nicknames for this town east of Seville give an idea of its chief glory and its biggest challenge. "The Town of Towers" refers to its 11 Baroque belltowers, all adorned with glazed tiles. "The Frying-Pan of Andalucía" is a reference to its searing summer temperatures, due to the fact that it's one of the few towns not built up a hill. Écija's archaeological museum is worth a visit. ◈ *Map D3 • Museo Histórico Municipal: Palacio de Benemejí, C/Cánovas del Castillo 4; 955 90 29 19; Open 10am–1:30pm & 4:30–6:30pm Tue–Fri, 10am–2pm & 5–8pm Sat, 10am–3pm Sun (Jun–Sep: 10am–2:30pm Tue–Fri, 10am–2pm & 8–10pm Sat, 10am–3pm Sun); Free*

La Campiña: Socialism versus Feudalism

The fertile Campiña valley has been in the hands of a few noble families since the Catholic Monarchs handed out huge tracts as fiefdoms. The people who worked the land were little more than serfs, a situation that still accounts for local poverty. In the village of Marinaleda, however, its mayor has created an island of social idealism, and has succeeded in wresting plots of property away from the landlords to be communally owned by the workers.

Palacio del Marqués de la Gomera, Osuna

Osuna

8 The enormously powerful Dukes of Osuna get the credit for endowing this town with exceptional architecture. The massive bulk of the Renaissance church, the Colegiata de la Asunción, dominates the scene; inside, there's an impressive painting of the Crucifixion by José de Ribera. The Universidad, also Renaissance, has tiled towers at its corners and a beautiful central courtyard. Elsewhere, fine mansions evoke the wealth of Spain's most powerful families *(see p38)*. ◈ *Map D4 • Colegiata: Plaza de la Encarnación; 954 81 04 44; Open May, Jun, Sep: 10am–1:30pm, 4–7pm Tue–Sun; Jul–Aug: 10am–1:30pm, 4–7pm Tue–Sat, 10am–1:30pm Sun; Oct–Apr: 10am–1:30pm, 3:30–6:30pm Tue–Sun; Adm*

Carmona

9 The closest major town east of Seville has been continuously inhabited for more than 5,000 years. Its Roman remains are truly exceptional, especially the huge necropolis. The view from the originally Roman Puerta de Córdoba (Córdoba Gate) out over the sweeping plains also shouldn't be missed. Fine churches, palaces and *alcázares* adorn the site – one of the ancient castles is now restored as a spectacular parador *(see p140).* ◈ Map C3 • Necrópolis: Avda Jorge Bonsor 9; 954 14 08 11; Open 9am–6pm Tue–Fri, 9:30am–2:30pm Sat & Sun; Closed public hols; Free

Itálica
10 These wind-blown ruins were once the third largest city in the Roman empire, founded in 206 BC and home to some half a million people during the reign of Emperor Hadrian in the 2nd century. He was following in the glorious footsteps of his predecessor Trajan, who was another Itálica native. There's a huge amphitheatre to explore, as well as some fine mosaics amid the crumbling walls. Most of the wonders are still buried, however, while others have long since been quarried for their stone or moved to the Archaeological Museum in Seville *(see p76).* ◈ Map B3 • Avda de Extremadura 2, Santiponce • 955 62 22 66 • www.junta deandalucia.es/cultura/museos • Open Apr–Sep: 8:30am–9pm Tue–Sat, 9am–3pm Sun; Oct–Mar: 9am–6:30pm Tue–Sat, 10am–4pm Sun • Adm (free for EU members)

Roman ruins, Itálica

A Day in Columbus's Footsteps

Morning

Head to the Monasterio de Santa María de la Rábida, 9 km (5.5 miles) from **Huelva City** *(see p87),* where a despondent Columbus found spiritual solace and practical help from the prior. The latter eventually persuaded Queen Isabel to sponsor the voyage that would discover America. The monks provide a tour *(10am–1pm, 4–7pm Tue–Sun (winter: to 6:15pm); Adm)* showing visitors where Columbus stayed. It's also a pleasant place for refreshment or a meal in the shaded café.

Below the monastery, on the waterfront, la **Muelle de las Carabelas** sports lifesize replicas of the three boats that made the trip *(see p62).*

Afternoon

Some 4 km (2.5 miles) northeast of La Rábida is the port, Palos de la Frontera, now silted up, from which Columbus set sail. More than half his crew also signed on here – the Iglesia de San Jorge is where the men heard mass before departing. Behind the church is La Fontanilla, the well that supplied them with water for the journey.

A further 7 km (4 miles) northeast is Moguer. Here, at the Convento de Santa Clara, Columbus gave thanks after his first voyage for having survived a storm in the Azores *(Tours 11am–7pm Tue–Sat; Adm).*

At the end of your circuit, relax over a meal at La Parrala *(Plaza de las Monjas 22, Moguer • 959 37 04 52 • Closed Mon • €€).*

If you don't have your own car, 10 bus trips make the Columbus circuit, from Huelva City to Moguer and back, Tue–Sat.

Left **Jabugo ham shop** Right **Almonaster La Real**

Best of the Rest

1 Aroche
Close to the Portuguese border, this town remains one of the best-preserved villages around. A wonderful oddity is the Museo del Santo Rosario, packed with rosaries that have belonged to Mother Teresa, John F Kennedy and General Franco, among others. ◈ *Map A2 • Museo del Santo Rosario: Paseo Ordoñez Valdés; Visit by appointment, 959 14 02 61; Free*

2 Niebla
Massive ramparts, built by the Moors in the 12th century, attest to the central role this town played in defending the land. The walls stretch for about 2.5 km (1.5 miles). ◈ *Map B4*

3 Cortegana
Dominated by a 13th-century castle, this is one of the largest towns in the area. ◈ *Map B3*

4 Almonaster La Real
A 10th-century mosque, a castle and a bullring are all clustered on the citadel overlooking the village *(see p42)*. ◈ *Map B3*

Ramparts, Niebla

5 Jabugo
The "home of ham" produces Spain's most famous, known as *jamón ibérico* (cured Iberian ham), *jamón serrano* (mountain-cured ham) and *pata negra*, named after the black pigs that forage in the Sierra de Aracena. ◈ *Map B3*

6 Aracena
Capital of the sierra, this is an attractive town blessed with fresh air. The oldest town hall in the province offers information about the sierra. ◈ *Map B3*

7 Parque de la Sierra de Aracena y Picos de Aroche
This wild area provides plenty of inspiring views and fauna *(see p44)*. ◈ *Map B2*

8 Santa Olalla del Cala
Set off by a 13th-century castle, this village lies in the heart of the ham-curing area. The 15th-century parish church has a fine Baroque interior. ◈ *Map B3*

9 Alájar
A picturesque hamlet of whitewashed buildings, cobbled streets and a Baroque church *(see p42)*. ◈ *Map B3*

10 Zufre
This cliff-top community is like a mini-Ronda *(see pp24–5)*. The Paseo de los Alcaldes has rose and lime trees and a mirador with views across the terraced plain. ◈ *Map B3*

Left **Mountain-cured ham** Right **Local ceramic dish**

🔟 Provincial Shopping

Aroche Markets
Thursday is the day the market stalls arrive in this Huelvan town. The market in Plaza de Abastos is a traditional produce spread, featuring the strong-flavoured goat's cheese favoured by the locals.

Souvenirs
In Aracena, head for the Calle Pozo de la Nieve, a cobbled street lined with souvenir shops. In El Rocío (see p87), souvenir stalls flank the church, hawking paraphernalia associated with the famous Romería (see p31).

Crafts
In addition to leather, Valverde del Camino is known for furniture and fine wooden boxes. Embroidery work from Aracena and Bollullos del Condado is worth seeking out, as well as linen tablecloths from Cortegana and Moguer. Nearer the coast it is also common to see Moroccan goods for sale.

Pottery
Pottery in this area has traditional patterns influenced by Moorish art. Items include jars, plates and water jugs, decorated in blue, green and white glazes.

Leather
The most notable leather goods come from Valverde del Camino. Choose botos camperos (cowboy boots) or the longer botos rocieros (Spanish riding boots). Many shops produce these items and other footwear, and a number of craftsmen make custom boots to order, taking three to four days to make a pair.

Huelva City
The provincial capital (see p87) boasts its own El Corte Inglés department store on Plaza de España, while the area around it and just off Plaza 12 de Octobre constitutes the main shopping district. The Mercadillo (open-air market) is held every Friday on the Recinto Colombino.

El Condado Wine District
The name refers to an area noted for its reliable white wine. Local finos include Condado Pálido and Condado Viejo.

Anise Liqueur
The liqueur of choice around this zone is anise-based. One of the best is Anis Cazalla from the eponymous town (see p88).

Ham
The Mesón Sánchez Romero Carvajal in Jabugo is one of the top producers of the local jamón ibérico (see p90).

Cured Fish
Considered a great delicacy and priced accordingly, raw wind-cured tuna (mojama) is an acquired taste. Isla Cristina is the main centre of production, but you can buy it in the Mercado del Carmen in Huelva City.

Left & Right **Casa Curro, Osuna**

🔟 Cafés and Tapas Bars

1 Bar Plaza, Carmona
In the heart of town, with terrace seating out in the square, this is a great little place for *tapas*. Go for the assortment menu if you want to be adventurous. One of the specialities is the rustic stew *pisto*, a concoction of vegetables with a poached egg. ⌘ *Plaza San Fernando 2; 954 19 00 67 • Map C3*

2 Bar La Reja, Écija
This local favourite offers a wide choice of *tapas* and *raciones* and the leisurely atmosphere invites sitting around and eaves-dropping on local gossip. ⌘ *C/Elvira 1; 954 83 30 12 • Map D3 • Closed Sun*

3 Casa Curro, Osuna
A few blocks from the main square, this is a premier *tapas* bar. It's diminutive, but worth seeking out for the quality. ⌘ *Plazuela Salitre 5; 955 82 07 58 • Map D4*

4 El Martinete, Cazalla
This minuscule bar is part of the facilities for a camp site. The plus here is that along with your reasonably priced *tapas* there are woods and waterfalls to enjoy. ⌘ *Ctra Estación de Cazalla km12; 955 88 65 33 (information) • Map C3 • Closed Mon*

5 La Puerta Ancha, Ayamonte
A sociable place that purports to be the original town bar. There are tables on the square and good prices, too, for their line of drinks, *tapas* and other snacks. ⌘ *Plaza de la Laguna 14; 959 32 19 96 • Map A4*

6 Espuma del Mar, Isla Canela
This beachside establishment has *al fresco* tables so you can people-watch while sampling tasty *tapas*. The speciality is, of course, fresh fish and seafood. Try *raya* (skate) in one of its various manifestations. ⌘ *Paseo de los Gavilanes; 959 47 71 98 • Map A4*

7 El Refugio, Mazagón
A laid-back, popular haunt in this surfer's paradise. Located a short stroll from the beach, El Refugio is renowned for its fresh fish dishes. ⌘ *Avda Santa Clara 43; 610 74 53 31 • Map B4 • Closed Mon–Thu (Oct–May)*

8 Bar Lalo, Aroche
A little bar with balconies looking on to the plaza. For something different try the local liqueur made from *bellotas* (acorns). ⌘ *Plaza Juan Carlos • Map A2*

9 Café Bar Manzano, Aracena
On the south side of the town square this traditional bar is a classic Sierra place for coffee and a pastry. ⌘ *Plaza del Marqués de Aracena 22; 959 12 81 23 • Map B3 • Closed Tue, last week Sep*

10 Hostería La Rábida
Next to an old monastery just east of Huelva where Columbus found spiritual retreat. You can have a drink or snack, or enjoy a full meal. ⌘ *Paraje de la Rábida; 959 350035 • Map A4 • Closed Mon and Jan*

Price Categories

For a three-course meal for one with half a bottle of wine (or equivalent meal), taxes and extra charges.

€	under €20
€€	€20–€30
€€€	€30–€40
€€€€	€40–€50
€€€€€	over €50

Above **Local seafood**

🔟 Restaurants

1 Restaurante San Fernando, Carmona

Carmona's classiest choice occupies an old mansion and overlooks the eponymous plaza. Expect fine service and a well thought out menu that features a range of local game, lamb, duck and fresh fish. Great desserts. ◈ *C/Sacramento 3 • Map C3 • 954 14 35 56 • Closed Sun D, Mon • €€€*

2 La Alquería, Sanlúcar la Mayor

Beautifully crafted delicacies can be enjoyed in the surroundings of a luxurious hotel housed in an 18th-century country estate. Smart dress. ◈ *Hacienda Benazuza, C/Virgen de las Nieves • Map B4 • 955 70 33 44 • Closed Mon, Sun • €€€€€*

3 Restaurante Doña Guadalupe, Osuna

A place to try *rabo de toro* (stewed bull's tail), game or *perdiz con arroz* (partridge with rice). Home-made desserts are a treat. ◈ *Plaza Guadalupe 6–8 • Map D4 • 954 81 05 58 • Closed Tue, 1–15 Aug • €€€*

4 Cambio de Tercio, Cazalla

This place is popular with devotees of rural cookery. Specialities include *solomillo de cerdo ibérico en salsa de setas* (Iberian pork loin in wild mushroom sauce) and for dessert *tarta de castañas* (chestnut tart). ◈ *C/Virgen del Robledo 53 bajo, Constantina • Map C3 • 955 88 10 80 • Closed Tue, last week Sep • €*

5 Mesón Las Candelas, Aljaraque

This attractive restaurant is the best for perfect seafood and fish. ◈ *Ctra Punta Umbria, Avda de Huelva • Map A4 • 959 31 83 01 • Closed Sun • €€€*

6 Restaurante Azabache, Huelva City

This traditional eatery is popular with locals and is known for its *raciónes*, or large servings of *tapas*. ◈ *C/Vázquez López 22 • Map A4 • 959 25 75 28 • Closed Sat D, Sun • €€*

7 Casa Luciano, Ayamonte

The place for tempting seafood and fish stews. Try the mouthwatering *atún al horno* (baked tuna). ◈ *C/Palma del Condado 1 • Map A4 • 959 47 10 71 • Closed during the Romería (see p31) • €€*

8 Aires de Doñana, El Rocío

French windows provide panoramic views of the marshes here. The *pato con arroz* (duck with rice) is a treat. ◈ *Avda La Canaliega, 1 • Map B4 • 959 44 27 19 • Closed Mon, 20 days in July • €€*

9 Asador Marisquería Picos de Aroche, Aroche

A wide variety of meat and seafood is on offer at this lovely grillhouse. ◈ *N433, km 127 Aroche • Map A2 • 959 14 01 87 • €*

10 Casa El Padrino, Alájar

This rustic favourite is known for its tasty regional cuisine. ◈ *Plaza Miguel Moya 2 • Map B3 • 959 12 56 01 • Closed Mon–Thu (except Aug) • €*

Note: *Unless otherwise stated, all restaurants accept credit cards and serve some vegetarian dishes such as salad or a* tapa

Left **Arcos de la Frontera** Right **Sherry barrels, Jerez de la Frontera**

Málaga and Cádiz Provinces

THESE TWO ANDALUCÍAN PROVINCES *are a heady mix of cultural and recreational riches seldom equalled elsewhere in the world. Europe's oldest city, Cádiz, is located here, but the presence of history is balanced by the hedonistic delights of the Costa del Sol and its fine beaches. Some of the region's most dramatic landscapes lure nature-lovers, while others are drawn by the charms of the famed* pueblos blancos *(white villages), the most renowned being stupendous Ronda, birthplace of that strongest of Spanish traditions, the bullfight. This is also the area that produces the world-famous fortified wines known as sherry, as well as the celebrated sweet wines of Málaga. Finally, Europe's southernmost point is located here, Tarifa, with views over to North Africa, and a stone's throw away, the Rock of Gibraltar, an eccentric enclave of Britishness on the Mediterranean coast.*

Antequera

🔟 Sights

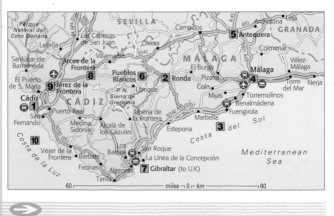

Cádiz

At the apex of the Atlantic's untamed Costa de la Luz (see p98), this city floats like an ancient dream on what was originally its own island. With good claim to being Europe's oldest city, it's thought to have been founded by the ubiquitous Phoenicians in around 1104 BC. Much of what can be seen today, however, dates from the 18th century, the city having been almost completely razed by an Anglo-Dutch raid in 1596. The vast Catedral Nueva (1722) is one of Spain's largest churches, and many Baroque edifices enhance this unpretentiously beautiful provincial capital and, apart from two weeks in February when it stages Spain's most celebrated Carnaval bash (see p60), it remains very much under-visited (see pp22–3).

Ronda

To many visitors over the centuries, this town evokes the "real" Andalucía, at its wild and scenic best. This mountain rock eyrie is quite literally

Puente Nuevo, Ronda

Nerja, Costa del Sol

breathtaking, being dramatically sliced down the middle by El Tajo, a fantastically deep and narrow limestone ravine, formed over thousands of years by the Río Guadalevín. The town itself is essentially two in one – the ancient half being steeped in rich Moorish history, with lovely cobbled streets, while the more modern part on the north side of the gorge sees to contemporary everyday needs (see pp24–5).

Costa del Sol

Still living up to its well-earned reputation as one of the world centres for sun, surf and cheap, superficial fun, this string of former Mediterranean fishing villages nevertheless retains more than at first meets the eye. To those who care to look beyond the brash tourist enclaves, there is still much authentic charm on offer here – and even a good share of places that offer the chance of tranquil reflection – especially in the towns of Estepona, Nerja, Mijas and ultra-classy Marbella (see p48). Year-round golf makes the whole area a great attraction for international lovers of the sport (see p103) and, in high season in particular, Torremolinos is the place to find some of Spain's liveliest nightlife (see pp26–7).

> *In early September Ronda's bullring stages the* Corridas Goyescas, *in which matadors fight in 18th-century style costumes.*

95

4 Málaga

Despite being home to the main airport bringing holiday-makers to the Costa del Sol, this provincial capital has been bypassed by the brunt of the "sun coast" development, and thus also by the swarms of foreign tourists. It has managed to hold onto its Spanish-ness quite admirably – despite attempts to bring it up to speed with the buzzing Costa lifestyle. An important trading port since ancient times, it was the favourite city of poet Garcia Lorca *(see p57)*, who loved it for its rawness. But its even greater claim to artistic fame is that it was the birthplace of Pablo Picasso, a fact that has now, at long last, been acknowledged by the presence of a Picasso museum, the third largest in the world dedicated to the modern master *(see p55)*. Málaga's alcázar, built between the 8th and 11th centuries, includes a Roman amphitheatre. ⊗ *Map E5 • Museo Picasso: C/San Agustín 8; 952 12 76 00; www.museopicassomalaga.org; Open Tue–Sun; Adm*

Setenil, a pueblo blanco

5 Antequera

So ancient that even the Romans called it Antiquaria, this market town presents a wonderfully condensed architectural history of the entire area, beginning with Neolithic dolmens dating from between 4500 and 2500 BC. In addition, there are significant Roman ruins, including villas with outstanding mosaics, a Moorish Alcazaba (closed to the public), the 16th-century Arco de los Gigantes, and fine Renaissance palaces and churches to explore. Many treasures originally found in the town – including the exquisite Ephebe of Antequera, a rare, life-size Roman bronze of a young boy – are displayed in the Municipal Museum, housed in an 18th-century palace. ⊗ *Map D4 • Museo Municipal: Palacio Nájera, Plaza del Coso Viejo, Closed until 2011*

6 Pueblos Blancos

The term "white villages" refers to the profusion of whitewashed hillside hamlets in the Serranía de Ronda, the mountainous territory around Ronda. Many of them are truly spectacular and it's well worth spending several days driving from one to the other, and then striking out on foot to take in some of the views *(see p52)*. Towns not to miss include Grazalema, Zahara de la Sierra, Gaucín, Casares, Setenil, Jimena de Libár and Manilva. Villagers, who originally settled on these plains to protect themselves from potential bandits in the lowlands, have lived the same way of life for centuries, and retain a strong agricultural tradition. Between Grazalema and Zahara, you'll go through

Gibraltar

Andalucía's highest mountain pass, the breathtaking Puerto de las Palomas (The Pass of the Doves). ◈ *Map C5*

7 Gibraltar

This gargantuan chunk of limestone rising up from the Mediterranean was one of the mythic Pillars of Hercules. Yet, despite being nicknamed "The Rock", as a worldwide symbol of stability and security, this fortress is actually a serious political football these days. Taken by the English in 1704 as part of the War of the Spanish Succession, today it is still very much a part of the British ethos, and only grudgingly do the Spaniards who live around it even acknowledge its existence. The Spanish government meanwhile most definitely wants it back. Legend has it that Britain will retain sovereignty of the rock as long as its most famous residents, the wild Barbary apes, remain, but their increasing number does not prevent ongoing diplomatic arguments. Still, if you're homesick for Englishness, cross over the frontier at La Línea to enjoy some fish and chips or a pint of ale. ◈ *Map C6*

A Morning Walk in Jerez de la Frontera

🕐 Begin your tour at the impressive alcázar, with its many Moorish remains, including restored gardens, a mosque and a *hammam* (baths), as well as a *camera obscura* providing views of the city and beyond. Beside it is the stunningly decorated cathedral, extravagantly rich inside and out. Note the fine painting of *The Sleeping Girl* by Zurbarán in the sacristy.

Next take the tour – with tastings – of the **González-Byass bodega** *(see p66)*, featuring possibly the oldest cellars in Jerez, with one designed by Gustave Eiffel. Don't miss the many signatures of famous people on the barrels (called "butts"), including Queen Victoria, Cole Porter, Martin Luther King and General Franco, among others.

Continuing on north, the **Pedro Domecq bodega** *(see p66)* also offers tours and is distinctively Moorish in style. A block further north, pop into the Museo Arqueológico to see the prized Greek bronze helmet from the 7th century BC, and then enter the Barrio de Santiago. This gently dilapidated neighbourhood of maze-like alleyways is home to a sizeable gypsy community and numerous flamenco venues.

To cap off your walk, continue straight out of the *barrio* to the east, past the Church of San Juan, to Restaurante Gaitán *(C/Gaitán 3 • 956 16 80 21 • €€€)* for a lunch of excellent Andalucían and Basque food.

Sherry, Brandy and Wine

The famed "Sherry Triangle" is comprised of the towns of Jerez, Sanlúcar de Barrameda and El Puerto de Santa María. The rich, nutty fortified wine has been produced here since ancient times, using vines imported by the Phoenicians some 3,000 years ago. In Roman times it was exported all over the empire, and it has been popular in England since the Elizabethan age. Sherry comes in a number of variants, to do with degrees of dryness or sweetness. The *fino* and *manzanilla* are dry and light, while the *amontillado* and *oloroso* are more robust. Brandy de Jerez is darker, richer and sweeter than brandy from France.

Arcos de la Frontera

Another town built atop a sheer cliff, this is probably the most dazzling of the *pueblos blancos* and the one situated furthest west. As ancient as any town in the region, little remains of the period before the *reconquista*, when it received its "de la Frontera" appellation, meaning it was a bastion "on the frontier" between Christian and Moorish Spain. The Galería de Arte Arx-Arcis crafts museum and shop displays locally fashioned carpets, blankets, baskets and pottery *(see p102)*. Map C5 • Galería de Arte Arx-Arcis: *C/Marques de Torresoto 11, 956 70 39 51; Open 10:30am–2:30pm, 5–9:30pm Mon–Sat; Free*

Jerez de la Frontera

The largest city in Cádiz province *(see p97)* is synonymous with the production of "sherry", which is simply a corruption of "Jerez" – itself a corruption of the original Phoenician name of Xeres *(see p67)*. Before that, it was part of the fabled Tartessian civilization (8th century BC). Sights include an array of religious edifices, various palaces and a rather academic archaeological museum. However, flamenco and horses also get the credit for bringing the city international fame. It has a renowned centre for equestrian art, Andalucían style, and is home to one of the largest remaining gypsy populations, a determining force in flamenco tradition *(see pp58–9)*. Map B5

Costa de la Luz

This stretch of Atlantic coast, named after its characteristic bright light *(luz)* and covering the area from Chipiona to Tarifa, is still off the beaten path despite attempts to exploit its wild loveliness. Part of what protects it are the prevailing winds, wonderful for windsurfers but wretched for sunbathers, who may have to face wind-tossed sands travelling at fairly high speeds. Still, there are excellent beaches that can be enjoyed, often backed by cliffs, and modest resorts, such as Chipiona *(see p99)*, mostly frequented by Spaniards. Map B5–C6

Costa de la Luz

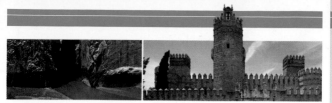

Left **El Chorro gorge** Right **El Puerto de Santa María**

🔟 Best of the Rest

1 El Torcal
A mountain nature reserve, great for hiking. The bizarre limestone rock formations are the big draw *(see p44)*. ◈ *Map D4*

2 El Chorro
A geographical wonder, the Chorro Gorge's immense gaping chasm, 180 m (590 ft) high, was created by the Río Guadalorce slashing through the limestone mountain. ◈ *Map D4*

3 Alcázar de Jerez
Jerez's Moorish fortress was originally part of a 4-km (2.5-mile) wall. A well-preserved mosque, now the Santa María La Real chapel, features an octagonal cupola over the *mihrab* (prayer niche). ◈ *Map B5 • Alameda Vieja • 956 31 97 98 • Open May–mid-Sep: 10am–8pm Mon–Sat, 10am–2:30pm Sun; mid-Sep–Apr: 10am–6pm daily • Adm*

4 Tarifa
The most southerly point of Europe, 11 km (7 miles) from Africa. Tarifa was the first town taken by the Moors in AD 710. Today it is a favoured spot for windsurfing. ◈ *Map C6*

5 Algeciras
Although the town of Algeciras is industrial and polluted, its port is the best in Spain; it is from here that you can catch the ferry to Morocco. It is fun to peruse the Moorish bazaars while waiting for the boat to take you across to the real thing. ◈ *Map C6*

6 El Puerto de Santa María
One of the towns of the Sherry Triangle. Several *bodegas* can be visited for tours and tastings *(see pp66–7)*. ◈ *Map B5*

7 Sanlúcar de Barrameda
Famed for its *manzanilla* sherry and superb seafood, the town also offers beautiful churches, palaces and tours of the *bodegas*. ◈ *Map B5*

8 Chipiona
This pretty resort town is crowded with Spanish beach enthusiasts in high season. The pace of life is leisurely, consisting of surf and miles of golden sand during the day, then strolls and ice cream until late in the evening. ◈ *Map B5*

9 Vejer de la Frontera
Of all the *pueblos blancos* *(see p96)*, this one has kept its Moorish roots most intact. Its original four Moorish gates still stand and its labyrinthine streets seem barely to have changed in 1,000 years. ◈ *Map C6*

10 Medina Sidonia
The most important edifice here is the 15th-century church of Santa María la Coronada, built over an earlier mosque. The interior features a 15-m (50-ft) high *retablo*. ◈ *Map C5 • Iglesia de Santa María la Coronada: Plaza Iglesia Mayor; 956 41 03 29, Open 10am–2pm, 4–8pm daily (summer), 10:30am–2pm, 4:30–7:30pm (winter); Adm*

Following pages: **Cádiz Cathedral**

Left **Hecho en Cádiz** Right **Mediterráneo**

TOP 10 Provincial Shopping

1 Málaga Wines
The Bodega El Pimpi in Málaga's old town is decorated like a traditional Andalucían house, together with wine barrels and pots of geraniums in the windows, while the walls display photos of all the celebrities who have been here. Choose from among the sweet wines of the Málaga area, based on the Moscatel and Pedro Ximénez grapes (see p67). ✆ C/Granada 68 • Map R5

2 Leather
In the shops of Ronda (see pp24–5) you'll find some of the best prices on leather goods of anywhere in Spain. Many of the items have well-known labels, since fashion houses often have contracts with leather factories in this area.

3 Mediterráneo, Cádiz
This is the best place in Cádiz to find provincial crafts. There's an excellent array of practical and decorative ceramics, rugs, blankets, ponchos, candles, jewellery and lots more, all at very affordable prices. ✆ C/San Pedro 12, 956 22 70 89 • Map B5

4 Hecho en Cádiz, Cádiz
Paintings and sculptures by local artists are available here, but they also carry a full line of gastronomic specialities from the area, including honey, wine, olive oil, as well as crafts of all sorts. ✆ Plaza Candelaria, 956 28 31 97 • Map B5

5 Los Duros Antiguos, Cádiz
This is the place for CDs of Carnaval music, videos of the zany goings-on, commemorative shirts and posters (see p60). ✆ C/Beato Diego de Cádiz, 956 21 11 68 • Map B5

6 Flamenco Costumes
One of the very best places to find genuine flamenco gear is Jerez de la Frontera. Head for Calle del Flamenco. ✆ Francos 49, Jerez, 956 34 01 39 • Map B5

7 Equestrian Equipment
Jerez is one of the best places in the world for refined horseriding gear. Arcab is a good starting point; it also has a branch on Paseo de Colón in Seville. ✆ Arcab: Avda Duque de Abrantes, Jerez, 956 32 41 00 • www.arcab.es • Map B5

8 Sherry
Jerez de la Frontera is, of course, also the prime spot to savour the finer points of a fino, a manzanilla, an amontillado or an oloroso (see pp66–7).

9 Traditional Textiles
The villages of Grazalema and Arcos de la Frontera (see p98) are known for their blankets, ponchos, rugs and other woven textiles.

10 Gibraltar Shopping
The shopping draw here is twofold: there's no sales tax and it's mostly duty-free and most UK high-street names are represented, such as The Body Shop and Marks & Spencer. ✆ Map C6

Sign up for DK's email newsletter on traveldk.com

Left & Right **Costa del Sol golf courses**

🔟 Costa del Sol Golf Courses

1 Valderrama
This is the most famous golf club along the Costa – it hosted the Ryder Cup in 1997. A Robert Trent Jones masterpiece and rated number one in continental Europe. ✆ *Ctra Cádiz-Málaga km132, Sotogrande • Map D6 • 956 79 12 00 • www.valderrama.com*

2 Real Club de Golf Sotogrande
Royal Sotogrande opened in 1964 and is still one of Europe's top 10 courses. Green-tee-paying visitors are welcome if they book in advance. The Robert Trent Jones design features mature trees and plenty of water obstacles. ✆ *Paseo del Parque, Sotogrande • Map D6 • 956 78 50 14 • www.golfsotogrande.com*

3 San Roque
Opened in 1990, San Roque is a Dave Thomas design. The course has been planned so that the holes are located in the same direction as the prevailing wind. ✆ *N-340 km126.5, San Roque • Map C6 • 956 61 30 30 • www.sanroqueclub.com*

4 Real Club Las Brisas
This is recognized as one of the finest courses in Europe. Also designed by Robert Trent Jones and opened in 1968, it has hosted the World Cup on two occasions and the Spanish Open three times. It features raised greens, numerous sand traps and water features. ✆ *Urb. Neuva (Andalucia), above Puerto Banús, Marbella • Map D5 • 952 81 08 75 • www.golf-andalucia.net*

5 Alcaidesa Links
The only links course in Spain opened in 1992, designed by Peter Alliss and Clive Clark. ✆ *N-340 km124.6, La Línea • Map C6 • 956 79 10 00 • www.alcaidesa.com*

6 Golf El Paraíso
This British-style golf club was designed by Gary Player. ✆ *Ctra N-340, km167, Estepona • Map D5 • 952 88 38 35 • www.elparaisogolfclub.com*

7 Los Arqueros
This was the Costa's first course to be designed by Spanish champ Seve Ballesteros. It offers a stiff test even for professionals. ✆ *Ctra de Ronda (A-397) km44.5, Benahavis • Map D5 • 952 78 46 00*

8 Miraflores
Designed by Folco Nardi, Miraflores has many challenging holes. ✆ *Riviera del Sol, Ctra de Cadiz km198, Mijas • Map D5 • 952 93 19 60*

9 La Duquesa
A Trent Jones design. The front nine holes begin in a westerly direction then finish with a long par five. ✆ *Urb. El Hacho, N-340 km143, Manilva (west of Estepona) • Map D5 • 952 89 07 25*

10 La Cañada
The long 1st hole sets the tone for a tough round of golf – the 4th is a trek into the unknown, with no view of the green until the third shot. ✆ *Ctra Guadiaro km1, Guadiaro, San Roque • Map C6 • 956 79 41 00 • www.lacanadagolf.com*

All golf courses charge a green fee that varies between €50 and €300. For course information: www.golf-andalucia.net

Left **Go-go dancers at a nightclub** Right **Olivia Valere**

Costa del Sol Nightlife

1 Olivia Valere, Marbella
This club is the Costa hot spot of the moment. Designed by the same creative genius who did Paris's famous Buddha Bar, it attracts the rich and beautiful like moths to the flame. Very exclusive and expensive. ⊗ *Crta de Istán, km0.8 • Map D5 • 952 82 88 61*

2 Ocean Club, Marbella
This chic club features a swimming pool and a VIP area with huge round beds. Enjoy a cocktail or sip champagne in the lounge. ⊗ *Avda Lola Flores • Map D5 • 952 90 81 37*

3 Suite, Marbella
This beachfront club has huge Buddhas, fire-eaters, belly dancers and jugglers. In the summer, the club becomes Suite del Mar and moves beachside, among palm trees. ⊗ *Puente Romano Hotel, Ctra de Cádiz km177 • Map D5*

4 Kiu, Benalmádena
This is the largest of the discos on this busy square. The Atlantis room is the best area for banging club tunes. ⊗ *Plaza Sol y Mar • Map D5 • 952 44 05 18*

5 Casino Torrequebrada, Benalmádena Costa
Located in the Hotel Torrequebrada, the casino has tables for blackjack, chemin de fer, punto y banco and roulette. The nightclub offers a flamenco show. Smart dress. ⊗ *Ctra de Cádiz • Map D5 • 952 44 60 00 • www.casinotorrequebrada.com*

6 Puerto Marina, Benalmadena
This large complex has a variety of bars, nightclubs, shops and restaurants. ⊗ *Puerto Marina • Map D5*

7 Mango, Benalmadena
Popular with the younger crowds, this club has an electric atmosphere. Most of its bars have a small dance floor and throbbing music. ⊗ *Plaza Solymar • Map D5*

8 Colonial Café, Marbella
At this large restaurant-cum-disco you can start the evening with a selection of *tapas* and dance the night away to various genres of music (house, soul, electronic, funk etc). ⊗ *Puerto Deportivo 13 • Map D5 • 685 87 14 87*

9 La Taberna de Pepe Lopez, Torremolinos
This flamenco venue is highly touristy, but fun. Shows take place here between 10pm and midnight every night. ⊗ *Plaza de la Gamba • Map E5 • 952 38 12 84 • Closed Sun*

10 Gay Torremolinos
Torremolinos has the hottest gay nightlife in the Costa del Sol. Start the night at trendy terrace bar El Gato (Nogalera 11), then head to Avda Palma de Mallorca for the best clubs. Popular spots include Sala Le Room (formerly Palladium, at No. 36) and Passion (No. 18). Minogues (in Montemar, near Benalmádena) hosts live drag shows. ⊗ *Map E5*

For Málaga and Nerja nightlife **See p106**

Price Categories

For a three-course meal for one with half a bottle of wine (or equivalent meal), taxes and extra charges.

€	under €20
€€	€20–€30
€€€	€30–€40
€€€€	€40–€50
€€€€€	over €50

Above **Bar Altamirano**

Costa del Sol Places to Eat

1 La Posá Dos, Estepona
Great Spanish food is featured here, with specialities such as roast lamb and the chef's own special creations. A romantic dinner choice. ✆ C/Caridad 95 • Map D5 • 952 80 00 29 • Closed L • €€

2 Bar Altamirano, Marbella
Despite Marbella's glitzy image there are several affordable and traditional *tapas* bars. This is one of them, just southeast of Plaza Naranjos; it even has its seafood specialities listed on ceramic menus. ✆ Plaza Altamirano 3 • Map D5 • 952 82 49 32 • Closed Wed, mid-Jan–mid-Feb • €€

3 El Estrecho, Marbella
Another winning *tapas* bar and a local favourite. There's a pleasant terrace, fish and seafood treats and nice *fino*. Try the *Boqueron al Limon* (Anchovies in Lemon). ✆ C/San Lázaro 12 • Map D5 • 952 77 00 04 • Closed first 2 weeks in Jun & Christmas • €

4 La Sirena, Benalmádena Costa
On the beachfront, and the paella is one of the best in the area. ✆ Paseo Marítimo • Map D5 • 952 56 02 39 • Dis. access • €€

5 Bodegas Quitapenas, Torremolinos
An excellent seafood *tapas* bar amid all the fast-food joints. Spanish seafood, including *pulpo* (octopus). ✆ C/Cuesta del Tajo 3 • Map E5 • 952 38 62 44 • No credit cards • €

6 Restaurante La Escalera, Torremolinos
A great little choice with dreamy views from its terrace. The inventive international menu includes curry soup with green peas. ✆ C/Cuesta del Tajo 12 • Map E5 • 952 05 80 24 • Closed Sun • Dis. access • €

7 Las Acacias, Málaga
This open-air beach café serves the coast speciality – *sardinas ensartadas* (sardines grilled on a skewer). ✆ Paseo Marítimo, El Pedregal 90 • Map E5 • 952 29 89 46 • €

8 El Tintero II, Málaga
Another open-air restaurant on the beach. There's no menu, so the waiter will tell you what's on offer – all fish, of course. ✆ Ctra Almería 99, Playa Del Dedo • Map E5 • 952 20 68 26 • Dis. access • €€

9 Restaurante Carabeo, Nerja
This café has been cut into the cliff, so you have views of the sea while protected under palm frond umbrellas. ✆ Mirador del Bendito, Edif. Rocomar 2 • Map E5 • 952 52 57 86 • €€

10 El Ancladero, Nerja
With another superb location on the cliff affording panoramic views of the sea, this place is a popular spot with photographers. The menu is eclectic, with the emphasis on steak and seafood. ✆ Capistrano Playa • Map E5 • 952 52 19 55 • Closed 21 Nov–7 Dec, 1–15 Jan • Dis. access • €€

Note: Unless otherwise stated, all restaurants accept credit cards and serve some vegetarian dishes such as salad or a tapa

Left **Las Bridas, Ronda** Right **Anfiteatro, Cádiz**

Nightlife in the Region

1 Varsovia, Málaga
This old-town disco attracts people of all ages. The music is a mix of 1980s feel-good, with some current hits thrown in. ✆ C/José Denis Belgrado 5 • Map R5

2 ZZ Pub, Málaga
Mostly university students come to this modest establishment in the old part of town, to hear the two regular bands that play here on Mondays and Thursdays. A DJ fills in the quiet moments every night. ✆ C/Tejón y Rodríguez 6 • Map Q4

3 Ronda After Dark
Café Las Bridas offers imported brews, with live music on weekends from midnight. Café Pub Dulcinea is a good place to dance to the latest Spanish electro-pop. ✆ Map D5 • Café Las Bridas: C/Remedios 18 • Café Pub Dulcinea: C/Rios Rosas 3

4 Nerja by Night
Funky beats and House music make Narixa a popular place to party. Coconut, on the other hand, is more laid back and is where you'll find the salsa crowd hanging out. ✆ Map E5 • Narixa: C/Tajillo • Coconut: C/Antonio Millón

5 Cádiz Pop
The zone around the harbour is loaded with venues and Anfiteatro is one of the best. Open Thursday to Saturday. ✆ Map B5 • Anfiteatro: Paseo Almirante Pascual Pery Junquera, 956 22 45 19

6 Cádiz Flamenco
The flamenco clubs burst with life in Cádiz. Good bets include Peña La Perla and Peña Enrique el Mellizo. ✆ Map B5 • Peña La Perla: C/Carlos Ollero • Peña Enrique el Mellizo: Punta San Felipe

7 Flamenco in Jerez
Here you will find genuine flamenco at its impassioned best. The gypsy quarter of Santiago is the place to make for, where you will find a number of *peñas* (clubs), but don't expect much before 10pm. ✆ Map B5

8 Tarifa Nights
You do not even have to leave the beach to check out the open-air Il Balneario. The floor is sand and the feel is tropical. In town, Tanakas can accommodate about 1,000 people. ✆ Map C6 • Il Balneario: Playa Chica • Tanakas: Plaza de San Hiscio

9 Gibraltar Nightlife
There are more than 360 pubs in Gibraltar. Those that enjoy late nights should visit Queensway Quay, Marina Bay and Casemates Square, which have a wide selection of bars, often with live entertainment. ✆ Map C6

10 Gibraltar Gambling
In addition to the bar scene, the Rock boasts the Ladbroke International Casino Club, which offers spectacular views over the bay and live entertainment. ✆ 7 Europa Road • Map C6

For nightlife and restaurants on the Costa del Sol **See pp104–105**

Price Categories

For a three-course meal for one with half a bottle of wine (or equivalent meal), taxes and extra charges.	
€	under €20
€€	€20–€30
€€€	€30–€40
€€€€	€40–€50
€€€€€	over €50

Above **El Faro, Cádiz**

🔟 Places to Eat in the Region

1. Ventorrillo del Chato, Cádiz

The oldest restaurant in Cádiz (1780), this inn on the Playa de Cortadura is also one of the best. Try *salmorejo*, a thick tomato soup served as a dip or side dish, and *dorada a la sal*, a local fish baked in a salt crust. ◎ Ctra Cádiz-San Fernando 2km (Via Augusta Julia) • Map B5 • 956 25 00 25 • Closed Sun D (all day in Aug) • €€€€

2. El Faro, Cádiz

This is probably the best place in Cádiz to enjoy fresh fish. *Lubina* (sea bass) is a perennial favourite, as are *cigalas* (giant crayfish). ◎ C/San Felix 15 • Map B5 • 956 22 19 59 • €€€

3. El Bosque, Jerez

In a town noted for elegance, its best restaurant is formal, as you would expect. It serves excellent seafood. ◎ Avda Alcalde Alvaro Domecq 26 • Map B5 • 956 30 70 30 • Closed Sun, Mon D • €€€

4. Bar Juanito, Jerez

This bar is famous for the best *tapas* in town. Try *fideos con gambas* (noodles with prawns). ◎ C/Pescadería Vieja 8 & 10 • Map B5 • 956 33 48 38 • Closed Sun D and during the May Feria • €

5. Casa Flores, El Puerto de Santa María

A stunning setting and the finest fresh seafood make this one of the best choices in this port town. ◎ C/Ribera del Río 9 • Map B5 • 956 54 35 12 • €€€

6. Tragabuches, Ronda

Probably the best restaurant in Andalucía. The chef has re-thought provincial cuisine and come up with a unique post-modern fusion. Choices include gazpacho ice cream and garlic soup with herring, egg and figs. ◎ C/José Aparicio 1 • Map D5 • 952 19 02 91 • Closed Sun D, Mon • €€€€

7. Tetería Al-Zahra, Ronda

In this authentic Moroccan-style tearoom sip mint tea – or slurp a milkshake – and delve into delicious Arab pastries. ◎ C/Las Tiendas 19 • Map D5 • 607 74 51 73 • Closed Tue • No credit cards • €

8. Bar La Farola, Ronda

This traditional *tapas* bar serves wonderful *chipirones* (baby squid), *berenjenas* (aubergine/eggplant) and mouth-watering *chorizos* (paprika sausages). ◎ Plaza Carmen Abela 10 • Map D5 • 952 87 15 47 • Closed Sun • €

9. Antigua Casa de Guardia, Málaga

The city's oldest *taberna*, dating from 1840. Some 20 barrels of local wine line the bar. The steamed mussels *(mejillones)* are great. ◎ Alameda Principal 18 • Map Q5 • 952 21 46 80 • Closed Sun • €

10. Antonio Martín, Málaga

The city's premier fish restaurant. *Fritura malagueña* (fish-fry Málaga-style) is popular. ◎ Plaza de la Malagueta s/n • Map S5 • 952 22 72 89 • €€€

Note: Unless otherwise stated, all restaurants accept credit cards and serve some vegetarian dishes such as salad or a tapa

Left **Monasterio de la Cartuja, Granada** Right **Cave dwellings, Guadix**

Granada and Almería Provinces

SO TAKEN ARE THEY WITH THE LEGENDARY PALACES OF THE ALHAMBRA, most tourists discover little else in these two provinces. However, besides numerous important and unique attractions in the enchanting city of Granada itself, the entire region is worth exploring, being especially rich in natural wonders. Spectacular mountains and superbly untouched coastal areas are the pride of both provinces, while inland some of the remote villages are among Andalucía's most fascinating and historic. Finally, film buffs will be delighted with the old "Spaghetti Western" movie sets that have been turned into endearingly quirky theme parks.

Moorish arch, Granada

🔟 Sights

1. Sierra Nevada
2. Moorish Granada
3. Cathedral & Capilla Real, Granada
4. Monasterio de la Cartuja, Granada
5. Museo-Casa Natal Federico García Lorca
6. Alhama de Granada
7. Almuñécar & Around
8. Guadix
9. Almería City & Around
10. "Wild West" Towns

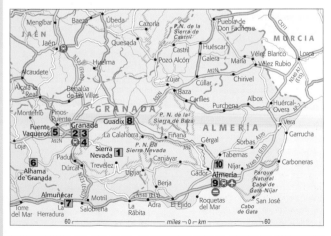

1 Sierra Nevada

Spain's tallest peaks – and, after the Alps, Europe's second-loftiest chain – make Andalucía home to some excellent skiing in winter and robust trekking in spring and summer, as well as abundant wildflowers and wildlife. For the more culturally inclined, the historic villages of the Alpujarras, on the southern slopes, are a fascinating study in an age-old way of life *(see pp32–3)*.

2 Moorish Granada

The fairytale palace of the Alhambra is one of Spain's main attractions, drawing millions of visitors each year. In the city below, the ancient Albaicín district embodies a microcosm of a North African village, a "Little Morocco", with colourful market streets and tearooms. Above and behind the area stands Sacromonte, the traditional home of cave-dwelling gypsies. Also worth a visit is the Museo Caja-Granada Memoria de Andalucía, devoted to Andalucian culture *(see pp8–13)*. ✎ *Map Q2 • Museo CajaGranada Memoria de Andalucía. Avda de la Ciencia 2; 958 22 22 57; Open 10am–8pm Tue–Sat, 10am–2pm Sun & public hols; Closed 1 Jan, 1 May, 25 Dec; Adm*

3 Cathedral & Capilla Real, Granada

To unequivocally establish Christian rule, these triumphalist structures were built by some of the greatest architects of the age and adorned with important works of art. The towering interior of Granada's cathedral is one of the most spectacular achievements of the period, while Alonso Cano's façade echoes the ancient triple arch favoured by Roman emperors. The Capilla Real (Royal Chapel) is Granada's finest Christian building and a repository of rare

Cathedral, Granada

treasures, including a *reja* (gilded grille) by Bartolomé de Jaén, priceless crown jewels, and paintings by Roger van der Weyden and Sandro Botticelli *(see p41)*. ✎ *Map Q2 • Catedral: C/Gran Vía de Colón 5; Open 10:45am–1:30pm & 4–7pm Mon–Sat (Apr–Oct: to 8pm; Jul & Aug: from 10am), 4–7pm Sun (Apr–Oct: to 8pm); Adm • Capilla Real: C/Oficios 3; 958 22 92 39; Open Apr–Oct: 10:30am–1pm & 4–7pm Mon–Sat, 11am–1pm & 4–7pm Sun; Nov–Mar: 10:30am–1pm & 3:30–6:30pm Mon–Sat, 11am–1pm & 3.30–6.30pm Sun; Adm*

4 Monasterio de la Cartuja, Granada

Don't let the austere exterior fool you – inside the church and sacristy of this Carthusian monastery lurk some of the most flamboyant Spanish Baroque architecture and detailing you'll ever encounter. So busy are the arabesques, flourishes and excrescences of gilded and polychromed stucco that the architectural lines are all but swallowed up in ravishing visual commotion. ✎ *Paseo de la Cartuja • Map F4 • 958 16 19 32 • Open Apr–Oct: 10am–1pm, 4–8pm Mon–Sat, 10am–noon, 4–8pm Sun; Nov–Mar: 10am–1pm, 3:30–6pm Sun, 10am–noon, 3:30–6pm Sun • Adm*

5 Museo-Casa Natal Federico García Lorca

Sadly, the many depths of Granada's talented native son – playwright, poet, artist, musician, impresario – were denied to the world when he was murdered at the age of 38 by Fascists at the beginning of the Spanish Civil War. His birthplace, in a village near Granada, has been turned into a museum devoted to his memory *(see p57)*. ✪ *C/Poeta García Lorca 4, Fuente Vaqueros • Map F4 • 958 51 64 53 • www.museogarcia lorca.org • Open for guided tours: 10am, 11am, noon, 1pm, 5pm & 6pm Mon–Sat; 10am & 11am Sun • Adm*

6 Alhama de Granada

Clinging precariously to the edge of a breathtaking gorge, this whitewashed village has been known since Moorish times for its beauty and natural thermal waters (*al-hamma* means "hot spring" in Arabic). The Hotel Balneario preserves the 11th-century *aljibe* (cistern), graced by Caliphal arches. In the 16th-century Iglesia de la Encarnación some of the priestly vestments on display are said to have been embroidered by Queen Isabel the Catholic. ✪ *Map E4*

Plasticultura

If you approach the coastal area of these provinces from the west, you will notice the extent of plastic tenting, a phenomenon that reaches a sea-like peak before Almería City. This agricultural technique is known as *plasticultura*, and is the last word in how to squeeze out every drop of moisture from these desert lands in order to produce crops.

The process is anything but organic, but this huge agribusiness does provide jobs, mostly for itinerant North Africans.

Castle overlooking Almuñécar

7 Almuñécar & Around

The Costa Tropical is perhaps Spain's most spectacular coast, where towering mountains rise from the shore. Almuñécar is the chief town along this stretch and it is now given over almost entirely to resort life. Yet it has an ancient heritage, dating back to the Phoenicians, and was an important port under the Moors. The intriguing Museo Arqueológico Cueva de Siete Palacios has a unique Egyptian vase dating from the 7th century BC *(see p55)*. ✪ *Map F5 • Museo Arqueológico Cueva de Siete Palacios: Barrio de San Miguel; 958 63 11 25; Open 10:30am–1:30pm & 5:30–8pm Tue–Sat, 10:30am–2pm Sun & public hols; Adm*

8 Guadix

This ancient town is famous for its cave dwellings, inhabited for centuries. They were developed after the *reconquista* by local Moors who had been cast out of society by the Christians. The Barrio de las Cuevas is a surreal zone of brown hills with rounded whitewashed chimneys sprouting up here and there. To learn more, visit the Cueva-Museo or instead stay in a cave hotel *(see p145)*. ✪ *Map F4 • Cueva-Museo: Plaza Padre Poveda, 958 66 55 69; www.cuevamuseoguadix.com; Open 10am–2pm & 4–6pm (5–7pm in summer) Mon–Fri, 10am–2pm Sat; Adm*

9 Almería City & Around

Notwithstanding its poetic Arabic name (*al-mariyat* means "mirror of the sea"), this town has lost much of its appeal due to modern development. Still, it does have a most impressive 10th-century Alcazaba, one of the most massive of the extant Moorish fortresses, and an engaging old quarter that still seems North African in essence.

⊛ *Map G4 • Alcazaba: C/Almanzor; Open Apr–Oct: 9am–8:30pm Tue–Sun (22 Jun– 1 Sep: to 11pm Fri & Sat); Nov–Mar: 9am– 6:30pm Tue–Sun; Adm*

10 "Wild West" Towns

The interior of Almería Province resembles the deserts and canyons of the American Southwest: it was the perfect spot for filming the Wild West epics known as "Spaghetti Westerns" in the 1960s and 1970s. Three of the sets are now theme parks: Mini Hollywood *(see p63)*, Texas Hollywood and Western Leone offer stunt shows and memorabilia.

⊛ *Mini Hollywood: Ctra N340 km 364, Tabernas; Map G4; 950 36 52 36; Open 10am–9pm daily (summer), 10am–7pm Sat–Sun & pub hols (winter); Adm • Texas Hollywood: Ctra N340 km 468, Paraje de Lunhay, Tabernas; Map G4; 950 16 54 58; Open Nov–Feb: 10am–6pm daily (Mar–Oct: to 9pm); Adm • Western Leone: Ctra A92, Tabernas; Map G4; 950 16 54 05; Open 10am–8pm daily; Adm*

Plaza Vieja, Almería City

A Morning in Granada

🕙 Begin your walk at Plaza Bib-Rambla, enhanced with flower stalls and the Neptune fountain. Fronting the western side of the square is the warren of ancient shopping streets called the **Alcaicería** *(see p114)*. Don't miss the 14th-century Moorish Corral del Carbón, which now houses craft shops and a cultural centre.

Once the **cathedral** *(see p109)* opens, it's time for a visit there; be sure to see the enormous Santiago el Matamoros (the Moor-slayer) on horseback, by Alonso de Mena, adorning the altar of St James. The next stop is the **Capilla Real** *(see p109)*; you should visit the crypt under the ostentatious marble sarcophagi of the kings and queens, where their bodies repose in plain lead boxes. On the carved Renaissance sepulchres, note the split pomegranate, symbol of a defeated Moorish Granada.

Continue on across the busy thoroughfares until you get to the river and the long expanse of the **Plaza Nueva** *(see p47)*. Choose an outside table (the cafés here are all similar), order a drink and take in the street life.

Now it's time to enter the labyrinth of the **Albaicín** *(see p12–13)*. Take Calle Elvira up to Calle Calderería Vieja for the vibrant bazaar of the Moorish Quarter. Following the old steep streets, keep going until you reach the fanciful **La Tetería del Bañuelo** *(see p116)*, an inviting place to sip some mint tea and sample Moroccan sweets.

➡ *Following pages:* **Albaicín quarter, Granada**

Left **Marquetry box, Granada** Right **Moroccan goods, Albaicín**

🔟 Traditional Handicrafts

1 La Alcaicería, Granada
In Moorish times this was the silk market, although the horseshoe arches and stucco work are a modern re-creation. The narrow alleyways are bursting with colourful wares of every description. Silver jewellery, embroidered silk shawls and ceramics are top buys. ◈ *Map Q2*

2 Albaicín, Granada
The authentic Moroccan shops in this ancient quarter are all concentrated on two sloping streets off Calle Elvira – Calderería Vieja and Calderería Nueva *(see pp12–13).*

3 La Alacena, Granada
This is a tempting place to come for regional foodstuffs. You'll find some of the finest olive oils, local and national wines and ham from the southern slopes of the Sierra Nevada. ◈ *Cuesta del Perro 5, 617 67 81 19 • Map F4*

4 Artesania Carazo Ortiz E, Granada
In this mystical place you can find the likes of handmade ceramics and natural stones, and you may even stumble upon some archeological items for sale. ◈ *C/Zacatín 11, 958 22 62 60 • Map R2*

5 Manuel Morillo Castillo, Granada
Arab-style furniture and *taracea* (marquetry) boxes are made and sold here *(see p64).* ◈ *Cuesta de Gomérez 20, 958 22 97 57 • Map R2*

6 El Rocío, Granada
The complete outfitter for *romería* and festival-going gear. All the frills, polka dots and bright colours will dazzle your eye, and it all comes in every size, so even babies can have a flounce or two. ◈ *C/Capuchinas 8, 958 26 58 23 • Map Q2*

7 Bazar el Valenciano, Almería
This is the oldest store in town. Look for "El Indalo" souvenirs, items bearing the symbol of Almería for good luck. ◈ *C/Las Tiendas 34, 950 23 45 93 • Map G4*

8 Artesania El Suspiro, Granada
A good array of all the traditional crafts that have survived in this city. Particularly appealing are the glazed tiles and the carpets in multicoloured designs. ◈ *Plaza Santa Ana 1, 958 22 99 96 • Map R2*

9 Alpujarras Crafts
The hill towns of this zone are rich in traditional crafts, including ceramics and weaving. Local *jarapas* (rugs) are particularly prized. Bags, ponchos and blankets, too, are hand-loomed in age-old patterns. They're sold at local weekly markets. ◈ *Map G4*

10 Níjar, Almería Province
This coastal town is known for its distinctive pottery and *jarapas*. Head for Calle Las Eras, in the Barrio Alfarero, just off the principal street, where you'll find the genuine article. ◈ *Map H4*

Left **Paña El Taranto** Right **Planta Baja**

⸿10 Nightlife

1 El Camborio, Granada
This is a popular disco in the caves of Sacromonte *(see p13)*. Music echoes from four dance floors to the rooftop terraces, offering a striking view of the Alhambra at sunrise. Weekends are the time to go, unless you want the place to yourself.
◈ *Camino del Sacromonte 48 • Map S1 • 958 22 12 15*

2 Granada 10, Granada
An opulent disco set in a 1930s theatre whose decor has been preserved. You can dance under crystal chandeliers, Neo-Classical-style plasterwork and plush private boxes. The music consists mainly of chart hits that attract people of all ages and styles. ◈ *C/Carcel Baja 3 • Map Q2 • 958 22 40 01*

3 Bar Pilar del Toro, Granada
Near Plaza Nueva, this bar is a popular spot with the well-heeled of Granada. The stunning interior has a secluded courtyard and comfortable rattan sofas.
◈ *C/Hospital de Santa Ana • Map R2 • 958 22 38 47*

4 Sala Príncipe, Granada
In this two-storey disco the music consists mainly of Spanish pop and salsa but the DJ takes requests. It's a popular place, decorated in rather vulgar imitation of the Nasrid palaces on the hill above. ◈ *Campo del Príncipe 7 • Map R3 • 958 22 80 88*

5 Planta Baja, Granada
A two-storey venue: the upper floor is a quiet bar; downstairs, the DJs play chart hits and everyone dances. ◈ *C/Horno de Abad 11 • Map F4 • 958 25 35 09*

6 Al Pie de la Vela, Granada
The crowd here is mostly male, young and cruisy, but it isn't exclusively gay, drawing a mixed crowd of locals and foreigners. ◈ *C/del Darro 35 • Map R2*

7 El Ángel Azul, Granada
This gay bar has a basement dance floor and curtained booths, as well as monthly drag shows and striptease contests.
◈ *C/Lavadero de las Tablas 15 • Map F4*

8 Sala Boss, Almería
At this large disco with multiple rooms, a line-up of different DJs and live performances attracts a mixed crowd.
◈ *Castro de Filabres 2 • Map G4*

9 Eshavira, Granada
This atmospheric club hosts flamenco, jazz and ethnic music concerts on Thursdays and Sundays. Decorated in Moorish style, the centuries-old water cistern has been transformed into a stage. ◈ *Postigo de la Cuna 2 • Map Q1*

10 Peña El Taranto, Almería
For lovers of real flamenco without tourist kitsch, this is the best place in the city *(see p59)*.

Left **Kasbah** Right **La Tetería del Bañuelo**

🔟 Tearooms and Tapas Bars

1 La Tetería del Bañuelo, Granada

A more relaxed and inviting place is hard to imagine. The little rooms and intimate niches are suffused with a gentle light, the air with the aromas of tea and flowers and the sound of songbirds. Try some exotic brews and sweets and enjoy unsurpassed views. ◎ *C/Bañuelo 5 • Map R2*

2 Kasbah, Granada

Relax amid the comforts of this candlelit café. Silky pillows and romantic nooks abound. You can try Arab pastries and a selection of Moroccan teas.
◎ *C/Calderería Nueva 4 • Map Q2*

3 Pervane, Granada

Near the top of this hilly street, this tearoom feels authentically Moroccan. Sit on cushions on the floor at one of the upper windows, sip your mint tea, and take in the colourful street life down below.
◎ *C/Calderería Nueva 24 • Map Q2*

4 La Esquinita, Granada

Small, atmospheric and sometimes claustrophobic. A speciality here is fried fish.
◎ *Campo del Príncipe • Map R3*

5 Antigua Bodega Castañeda, Granada

Rows of antique wine barrels create the atmosphere here. The cheese boards are a good bet, as well as *montaditos* (small open sandwiches). ◎ *C/Elvira 5 • Map Q2*

6 Casa Enrique, Granada

This is another wonderfully old-fashioned hole-in-the-wall lined with antique barrels. Try the *montaditos de lomo* (little sandwiches with pork fillet) and *tarta de casar* (cheesecake). ◎ *C/Acero de Darro 8 • Map Q3*

7 Tetería Al Hammam Almeraya, Almería

Escape from the crowds of the town centre and head for the tranquil tearoom of Almería's Arab baths, where you can enjoy Moorish-inspired teas and snacks.
◎ *C/Perea 9 • Map G4 • Closed Tue*

8 Bodega Francisco, Almuñécar

A forest of ham shanks hanging from the ceiling greets the eye, along with barrels of *fino* behind the bar in this traditional *tapas* bar. The attached restaurant next door, Francisco II, serves full meals. ◎ *C/Real 14 • Map F5*

9 Casa Puga, Almería

One of the city's best *tapas* bars. The wine list is exhaustive, as you might guess from the many wine racks on view.
◎ *C/Jovellanos 7 • Map G4*

10 El Quinto Toro, Almería

The name derives from the tradition that the best bull of a *corrida* is chosen to fight in the fifth *(quinto)* confrontation of the day. This *tapas* bar is favoured by local aficionados of the bullfight. ◎ *Juan Leal 6 • Map G4*

Above **Arrayanes**

Price Categories

For a three-course meal for one with half a bottle of wine (or equivalent meal), taxes and extra charges.	€ under €20
	€€ €20–€30
	€€€ €30–€40
	€€€€ €40–€50
	€€€€€ over €50

🔟 Restaurants

1 Cunini, Granada
The fresh seafood, brought in daily from Motril, is highly recommended. It's a big hit with the food critics – so it must be good. ✆ Plaza Pescadería 14 • Map F4 • 958 25 07 77 • Closed Sun D, Mon • €€€

2 Arrayanes, Granada
The most authentic and sophisticated of the North African restaurants in the little Moroccan quarter. Only halal meat is served, and no alcohol. ✆ Cuesta Marañas 4 • Map Q2 • 958 22 84 01 • Closed Tue • €

3 Mirador de Aixa, Granada
With its position at the top of the Albaicín there are views of the Alhambra from the terrace. The food, too, is an adventure in local culture, featuring recipes such as habas con jamón (broad beans with ham). ✆ Carril de San Agustín 2 • Map Q2 • 958 22 36 16 • €€€€

4 Restaurante El Ventorro, Alhama de Granada
In this lovely rural restaurant you can try choto al ajillo (kid cooked with garlic) and bacalao con naranja (cod with oranges). ✆ Ctra de Jatar, km2 • Map E4 • 958 35 04 38 • Closed Mon • €

5 Restaurante González, Trevélez
In this famous ham town you'll get what you came for – the dining room is hung with legs of meat. ✆ Plaza Francisco Abellán • Map F4 • 958 85 85 33 • €

6 Jacquy Cotobro, Playa Cotobro, Almuñécar
One of Andalucía's finest restaurants. Belgian chef Jacques Vanhoren blends the best of his native cuisine with high points of Spanish cookery. ✆ Edificio Río Playa Cotobro 1 • Map F5 • 958 63 18 02 • Closed Mon (winter) • €€€€

7 El Tinao del Mar, La Herradura
Regional cooking at its simple best, which means seafood at this beach location. ✆ Edificio Bahía II, Paseo Marítimo de Don Andrés Segovia 17 • Map F5 • 958 82 74 88 • €€

8 Pesetas, Salobreña
Absorb the ambience of the old quarters of Salobreña and the excellent views of the coast while dining here. The choco a la mariñera (squid in tomato sauce) is a speciality. ✆ C/Bóveda 11 • Map F5 • 958 61 01 82 • €

9 Restaurante Valentín, Almería
Specialities include arroz negro (rice in squid ink) and pescado en adobo (clay-baked fish). ✆ C/Tenor Iribarne 19 • Map G4 • 950 26 44 75 • Closed Mon, Sep • €€€€

10 La Goleta, San Miguel del Cabo de Gata
All the seafood is at its freshest here, of course, since this village is located right in the middle of Andalucía's most unspoilt coast. ✆ Beachfront • Map H5 • 950 37 02 15 • Closed Nov & Mondays, Dec–May • €€

Note: Unless otherwise stated, all restaurants accept credit cards and serve some vegetarian dishes such as salad or a tapa

Left **Castillo de Almodóvar del Rio** Right **Montilla vineyards**

Córdoba and Jaén Provinces

THESE TWO PROVINCES ARE AN ATTRACTIVE BLEND *of exquisite urban architecture, famed agricultural zones and great wildlife reserves within rugged mountain ranges. The ancient treasure-trove of Córdoba City is the star, of course, but the Renaissance towns of Baeza and Úbeda are among the region's most beautiful. For wine-lovers and those who appreciate delicious ham and perfect olive oil, the areas around Montilla, Valle de los Pedroches and Baena should not be missed. Meanwhile, along the northern zones, nature lovers can hike for days and days amid the pristine wilds of the Parque Natural de la Sierra de Cardeña y Montoro in Córdoba Province and the Sierra de Cazorla in Jaén Province.*

Medina Azahara

🔟 Sights

1. Córdoba City
2. Úbeda
3. Baeza
4. Medina Azahara
5. Castillo de Almodóvar del Rio
6. Montoro
7. Valle de los Pedroches
8. Montilla
9. Jaén City
10. Alcalá La Real

Sign up for DK's email newsletter on traveldk.com

Córdoba City

This town, wonderfully rich in history and cultural importance, is also small enough to cover easily and enjoyably on foot. It has a delightfully contrasting mix of sights, from the architectural splendour of the great mosque – with a Christian church

Alcázar, Córdoba City

oddly sprouting out of its centre – to the whitewashed glories of the old Jewish quarter, the splendid Alcázar, and the frankly morbid museum dedicated to the bullfight. There are other engaging museums as well, featuring works of art by both Old Masters and local artists, and ancient artifacts evoking the area's influential past *(see pp18–21)*.

Úbeda

Ignore the downtrodden outskirts as you approach this town – once you get to the historic centre you will realize that it is one of Andalucía's most remarkable splendours. The keynote here is architecture – an entire district of mostly Renaissance edifices built for local nobility in the 16th century. One of Andalucía's greatest architects, Andrés de Vandelvira, was the genius who gave most of these structures their harmonious forms *(see pp28–9)*.

Renaissance church altar, Úbeda

Baeza

Like nearby Úbeda, this smaller town is also a jewel of Renaissance glory, but includes earlier remains dating back to the Moors and, before them, the Romans. The town radiates a sense of tranquillity as you walk from one cluster of lovely buildings to another. Again, much of the beauty owes its existence to Vandelvira *(see pp28–9)*.

Medina Azahara

The building of the first palace here dates from AD 936, commissioned by Caliph Abd el-Rahman III, Emir of Córdoba and the man who brought the city to glory. He named it after his favourite wife, Az-Zahra (the Radiant). Though it is little more than a ruin now – sacked in 1009 and rediscovered only in 1910 – at one time this pleasure-dome incorporated a zoo, ponds and gardens, baths, houses, barracks, markets, mosques, a harem of 6,000 women and accommodation for 4,000 slaves. Decorated with ebony, ivory, jasper and marble, it even had a pool of mercury that created dancing lights on the walls and ceiling. ✆ *Ctra Palma del Río km 5.5, W of Córdoba • Map D3 • 937 35 55 06 • Open 10am–8:30pm (to 6:30pm in winter) Tue–Sat, 10am–2pm Sun • Adm (free for EU members)*

Baena Olive Oil

It was the Romans who brought cultivation of the olive here, and the Moors who carried the tradition forward. This Córdoba Province town is famed for its olive oil, and you can catch its unmistakable fragrance as you enter the district. The Museo del Olivar y el Aceite *(C/Cañada 7 • 957 69 16 41 • Open Tue–Sun • Free)* is well worth a visit. It shows how each organically grown olive is carefully kept from bruising and the paste is extracted by the process of stone-crushing, the oil then being bottled and sealed in with wax.

5 Castillo de Almodóvar del Río

Originally the site of a Roman fortification, the present fairytale castle goes back to the 1300s, when it was embellished in Gothic style. Before that, it had been a Moorish structure dating from AD 740 that had survived four centuries of Christian sieges. The views from the battlements take in the whitewashed town below. Legend holds that ghosts of those who died while imprisoned here haunt the eight monolithic towers. ✎ *Map D3 • 25 km (16 miles) W of Córdoba; 957 63 40 55 • Open 11am–2:30pm & 4–7pm Mon–Fri (to 8pm in summer), 11am–7pm Sat & Sun (to 8pm in summer) • Adm*

Local produce, Valle de los Pedroches

6 Montoro

Attractively laid out on an undulating series of five hills at a bend in the river, this ancient town sports a Baroque tower and a handsome 15th-century bridge. Other sights include a good Museo Arqueológico Municipal and the eccentrically kitsch Casa de las Conchas, a shell-encrusted folly that the owner will be happy to show you around. ✎ *Map E2 • Museo Arqueológico: Plaza de Santa María de la Mota; 957 16 00 89; Open 11am–1pm Sat, Sun & pub hols; Free • Casa de las Conchas: C/Criado 17; Adm*

7 Valle de los Pedroches

The far north of Córdoba Province is fertile grazing land for farm animals, as well as deer and wild boar. Most importantly, it is a "land of acorns", densely clad with holm oaks and therefore a prime zone for raising the famed Iberian black pig. In October, the creatures are fattened up on acorns and their meat is elaborately cured to produce succulent *jamón ibérico* or *pata negra*, the local product rivalling that of Jabugo in Huelva Province. ✎ *Map D2*

8 Montilla

This town is the centre of Córdoba's wine-making region, where the word *amontillado* originates, meaning "in the style of Montilla". The wine produced here is like sherry, but nuttier and more toasted – and since the region is hotter than around Jerez, the grapes ripen more intensely and the wines need no fortifying. You can taste the difference for yourself at Bodegas Alvear *(see p66)*. ✎ *Map D3 • Bodegas Alvear: Avda de María Auxiliadora 1, 957 66 40 14; Open for tours in English 12:30pm Mon–Fri; by appt Sat, Sun & pub hols (for groups of 7 or more); Adm*

Cathedral, Jaén City

9 Jaén City

This modern provincial capital is set off by the dramatically placed ramparts of the mighty Castillo de Santa Catalina *(see p39)*, originally Moorish, and the immensity of its double-towered cathedral by Vandelvira *(see p41)*. You can fully experience the castle and its spectacular views of the city and surrounding olive groves, as it now houses a parador *(see p140)*. Another rewarding stop is the Museo Provincial, especially to see the country's finest collection of 5th-century BC Iberian sculpture. ◎ Map E3 • Cathedral: Plaza Santa María; Open 8:30am–1pm & 5–8pm Mon–Sat, 9am–1pm & 6–8pm Sun (only am Sun in summer); Free • Museo Provincial: Paseo de la Estación 27; Open 2:30–8:30pm Tue, 9am–8:30pm Wed–Sat, 9am–2:30pm Sun; Adm (free for EU members)

10 Alcalá La Real

The Fortaleza de la Mota that dominates this once strategic town is unique in Jaén Province in that its original Moorish castle was built by the rulers of Granada. It is mostly in ruins now, but it still preserves the original seven gates. Inside, built on the remains of a former mosque, is the Gothic-Mudéjar church of Santo Domingo, which uses the former minaret as a belltower *(see p38)*. ◎ Map E3 • Fortress: 639 64 77 96; Open 10:30am–1:30pm & 5–8pm daily (summer), 10:30am–1:30pm & 3:30–6:30pm daily (winter); Adm

A Morning Walk Through Baeza

Start your tour of this Renaissance town at the lovely **Plaza del Pópulo** *(see p28)*, where the tourist office is located in a fine Plateresque palace, the Casa del Pópulo. Next to it are the arches of the **Puerta de Jaén** *(see p28)* and the Arco de Villalar, while adorning the centre of the plaza is the Fuente de los Leones. The ruined lions and their eroded mistress, said to be a statue of Hannibal's wife, still manage to convey an undeniable elegance.

Exiting the square to the left of the tourist office, continue southeast to the **Plaza Santa María** *(see p28)* and the cathedral. Note the graffiti in bull's blood on the old seminary wall. Inside the cathedral, don't miss the extravagant choir screen by Bartolomé de Jaén.

Next stop, to the north, is the **Palacio de Jabalquinto** *(see p29)*, with one of the most eccentric façades in the region, an example of Isabelline Plateresque style. Visit its inner patio and then that of the Antigua Universidad next door. Down the street, you can see the 1,000-year-old Moorish Torre de los Aliatares and around the corner, facing **Paseo de la Constitución** *(see p29)*, La Alhóndiga, the old corn exchange, with its triple-tiered façade.

Have lunch at an outdoor table of the Restaurante Sali across from the town hall, which offers a range of choices from local farms *(Pasaje Cardenal Benavides 15 • 953 74 13 65 • Closed Wed D • €€)*.

Left **Arte Cordobés** Right **Traditional Córdovan olive oil**

🔟 Shops and Markets

1 Arte Cordobés, Córdoba
A good choice for traditional Córdovan silver. Everything from small sculptures to filigree jewellery is on offer. Gold filigree creations are available as well. ✎ *C/Deanes 17 • Map D3 • 957 47 76 87*

2 Ghadamés, Córdoba
Here, Córdoba leather is worked and coloured into traditional patterns and images, most of them relating to the area's Moorish history, although some are on religious themes and others pertain to local customs. ✎ *Corregidor Luis de la Cerda 52 • Map D3 • 957 48 16 07*

3 Bodegas Mezquita, Córdoba
This is an excellent place for local foodstuffs. Slow-cured hams, fine wines, olive oils and other delectables will tempt your palate. Their superb *tapas* bar is next door. ✎ *Corregidor Luis de la Cerda 73 • Map D3*

4 Baraka, Córdoba
For good-quality souvenirs this is likely spot. Choose from ceramics, leather goods, glassware and other accessories, all handmade. ✎ *C/Manriquez • Map D3 • 957 48 83 27*

5 Artesania Nuevo Mundo, Córdoba
This creative ceramic workshop and exhibition space offers courses and undertakes custom work. ✎ *C/Abogado Enriquez Barrio 2 • Map D3 • 957 41 41 47*

6 Monsieur Bourguignon, Córdoba
A decadent shop offering an assortment of chocolates and handmade sweets, which are almost too pretty to eat. ✎ *C/Jesús y María 11 • Map D3 • 656 33 02 80*

7 Nuñez de Prado, Baena
One of the premier olive oil factories in this historic town *(see p120)*. Their production methods have not compromised with modernity, so their oil remains rich and flavourful. ✎ *Avda de Cervantes • Map E3 • 957 67 01 41*

8 Galería de Vinos Caldos, Jaén
One of the region's best wine shops. Featured, of course, are regional wines, including those from Montilla *(see p120)*. ✎ *C/Ceron 12 • Map F3 • 953 23 59 99*

9 Flea Market, Jaén
Thursday mornings see this street come to life with a catch-all market that can net you anything from pure junk to a rare treasure. ✎ *Recinto Ferial, Avda de Granada • Map F3*

10 Pottery Quarter, Úbeda
Úbeda is famous for its dark green pottery, fired in wood kilns over olive stones. Its intricate pierced designs are Moorish-inspired and the workmanship superb. ✎ *C/Valencia • Map F2*

Price Categories

For a three-course meal for one with half a bottle of wine (or equivalent meal), taxes and extra charges.	€ under €20
	€€ €20–€30
	€€€ €30–€40
	€€€€ €40–€50
	€€€€€ over €50

Above **El Churrasco**

Top 10 Places to Eat

1 Tene2res, Jaén
This restaurant is part of a hotel complex in the heart of Cazorla. Regional fare is served, with samplings of local game and fish. ◈ *Magistrado Ruiz Rico 3, Cazorla (Jaén)* • Map G3 • *953 12 40 34* • €€

2 Taberna Sociedad de Plateros, Córdoba
Housed in a former convent, this *taberna* has a skylit patio decorated with *azulejos* (glazed tiles) and hanging plants. ◈ *C/San Francisco 6* • Map D3 • *957 47 00 42* • Closed Sun (summer), Mon (winter) • No credit cards • €

3 Taberna Salinas, Córdoba
A bustling place, with dining rooms around a patio. Try the *naranjas picás con aceite y bacalao* (cod with orange and olive oil). ◈ *C/Tundidores 3* • Map D3 • *957 48 01 35* • Closed Sun, Aug • €

4 Casa Rubio, Córdoba
Built into the old city wall, just inside the Judería, with Moorish arches and a stone floor, this atmospheric bar offers a good range of *tapas*. ◈ *Puerto Almodóvar 5* • Map D3 • *957 42 08 53* • €€€

5 El Churrasco, Córdoba
One of the city's smartest eateries, serving traditional fare in a sumptuous setting. Try the eponymous *churrasco* (grilled pork loin with spicy red pepper sauce). ◈ *C/Romero 16* • Map D3 • *957 29 08 19* • Closed Aug • €€€€

6 Almudaina, Córdoba
Set in a 16th-century mansion, this is another great place to try traditional dishes, such as *pochuga de perniz en salsa* (partridge breasts in sauce). ◈ *Plaza Campo Santo de los Martires 1* • Map D3 • *957 47 43 42* • Closed Sun D • €€€

7 Las Camachas, Montilla
Fish dishes are a speciality here, such as *lomos de merluza con almejas y gambas* (hake loin with clams and prawns). Wash it all down with a bottle of the delightful local wine. ◈ *Ctra Madrid-Málaga, Avda de Europa 3* • Map D3 • *957 65 00 04* • €€€

8 Taberna La Manchega, Jaén
An animated and authentic *tapas* bar. Downstairs they serve full meals, highlighting local meats. ◈ *C/Bernardo López 8 & Arco de Consuelo* • Map F3 • *953 23 21 92* • Closed Tue, Aug • No credit cards • €

9 Restaurante Andrés de Vandelvira, Baeza
Housed in a section of the eponymous architect's 16th-century Convento de San Francisco, dishes include *trucha escabechada* (marinated trout). ◈ *C/San Francisco 14* • Map F2 • *953 74 81 72* • Closed Mon • €€

10 Mesón Navarro, Úbeda
Something of a local institution. Try *pinchitos* (kebabs) and *ochios* (rolls). ◈ *Plaza Ayuntamiento 2* • Map F2 • *953 79 06 38* • €€

Note: Unless otherwise stated, all restaurants accept credit cards and serve some vegetarian dishes such as salad or a tapa

STREETSMART

ANDALUCÍA'S TOP 10

Left **Tourist office** Right **Enjoying the warm climate**

Planning Your Trip

1 Internet Information

There are several sources of information on the Internet. If you're interested in a particular place or aspect of the region, see the following websites for more information. ⊗ www.andalucia.com • www.andalucia.org • www.okspain.org • www.spain.info

2 Climate

The region enjoys a very mild climate. The year-round average temperature is 18–20°C (64–68°F) with some 320 sunny days. Coastal areas have highs fluctuating between 15°C (59°F) and 30°C (86°F). Inland, average city highs vary from 12°C (54°F) in January to 36°C (97°F) in August.

3 When to Go

Every season offers its reasons to come here: summer for nightlife, spring and autumn for nature, winter for skiing. But autumn is the best time – the weather is still good, the water is warm, the crowds have gone, prices are lower and there are lots of local festivals.

4 Passports & Visas

Britons and EU citizens have unlimited stay; Americans, Australians, New Zealanders and Canadians need only a valid passport to stay for 90 days. Other nationalities must get a visa from their Spanish consulate.

5 Spanish Embassies & Consulates Abroad

If you have any questions, your local Spanish embassy or consulate is well equipped to help you. ⊗ Australia: 15 Arkana St, Yarralumla, Canberra; 02 6273 3555 • Canada: 74 Stanley Ave, Ottawa; (613) 747 2252 • Ireland: 17a Merlyn Park, Dublin 4; (3531) 260 8066 • UK: 39 Chesham Place, London; 020 7235 5555 • USA: 2375 Pennsylvania Ave NW, Washington, DC; (202) 728 2340

6 Foreign Consulates in Andalucía

For any further questions whilst in Spain, contact your country's consulate. ⊗ Canada: Edificio Horizonte, Plaza de la Malagueta 3, Málaga; 952 22 33 46 • Ireland: Avda de los Boliches 15, Fuengirola; 952 47 51 08 • UK: Edificio Eurocom Sur, C/Mauricio Moro Pareto 2, 2°, Málaga; 952 35 23 00 • USA: Plaza Nueva 8-8 Duplicado, 2-E2, n4, Seville; 954 21 85 71

7 Spanish National Tourist Offices

This service (see box) will provide maps and brochures on request.

8 General Information

The time zone is that for Western Continental Europe (GMT +1 hour). Voltage is 220, and round-pronged plugs are used. UK gadgets need an adapter; US counterparts also require a transformer. The minimum age for driving is 18.

9 Insurance

It is always a good idea to obtain private medical insurance. Then, if you require treatment while on holiday, you pay for the care, keep the receipts and are reimbursed according to the terms of your policy. General travel insurance is also recommended.

10 What to Take

Casual dress is generally acceptable throughout Andalucía – linens or cottons are the best way to beat the summer heat. A hat will also be useful, and don't forget a high-factor sunscreen.

Spanish National Tourist Offices

Canada
2 Bloor St W,
34th Floor, Toronto
• (416) 961 3131

UK
2nd Floor,
79 New Cavendish St,
London W1W 6XB
• 020 7486 8077

USA
666 5th Ave,
35th Floor, New York
• (212) 265 8822

ONLINE INFO
www.spain.info

Check that an establishment's website is up to date before relying on the information supplied (prices, opening hours, etc).

Left **Cultural tour** Right **Andalucían bodega**

Specialist Holidays

1 Walking & Hiking Tours
Walking and hiking are up-close ways to explore the countryside, and many companies offer well-organized groups. ⊗ *Federación Española de Deportes de Montaña, Granada; 958 29 13 40*
• *Explore Worldwide, Farnborough (Hampshire); 08450 131 539*
• *Nevadensis, Pampaneira (Granada); 958 76 31 27; www.nevadensis.com*

2 Horse-Riding & Nature Tours
Nature lovers can take to trails on horseback, peer at the local birdlife from special hides, see the dolphins at the Straits of Gibraltar, or go on a nature safari. ⊗ *Bird Holidays, Yeadon, Leeds; 0113 391 0510; www.bird holidays.co.uk* • *Dolphin Safari, Marina Bay, Gibraltar; (350) 2007 1914* • *Rancho Los Lobos, Jimena de la Frontera (Cádiz); 956 64 04 29; www.rancholoslobos.com* • *Safari Andalucía, Gaucín (Málaga); 952 15 11 48*

3 Bodega Tours
Tours of the wine cellars *(bodegas)* in the Sherry Triangle and Málaga can be arranged either on the spot or in advance. Tours often feature samplings of the wines as well as gastronomic delights. ⊗ *Spanish Fiestas, Urb. Lindaraja 12, Almuñécar; 680 22 69 30* • *Saranjan Tours, Kirkland, Washington, USA; 800 858 9594*

4 Flamenco Tours & Salsa Holidays
Learn to dance, Spanish-style. The flamenco-based *sevillana* is a must for fiesta-goers, while the salsa is popular at clubs. ⊗ *Taller Flamenco, C/Peral 49, Seville; 954 56 42 34; www.tallerflamenco. com* • *Dance Holiday, 24–32 Stephenson Way, London; www.dance holidays.com*

5 Spanish Language Holidays
Combining a holiday with courses in Spanish is a popular choice. Schools often offer a range of other activities. ⊗ *Instituto Cervantes, 102 Eaton Sq, London; 020 7235 0353; www.londres.cervantes.es* • *Don Quijote, Azhuma 5, Granada; 923 27 22 00; www.donquijote.org* • *Instituto de Español Picasso, Plaza de la Merced 20, Málaga; 952 21 39 32*

6 Cultural Study Holidays
Many companies organize art, architecture and archaeology tours, or courses on regional cookery, painting and more. ⊗ *Responsible Travel.com, Pavilion House, 6 Old Steine, Brighton, UK; 01273 600030; www.responsible travel.com* • *Spain Dreams, Georg Buech, Badia 24, 4-2a, Barcelona; 93 53 09 426; www.spaindreams.com* • *Europa Photogenica, 3920 W 231st Place, Torrance, CA, USA; 310 378 2821; www. europaphotogenica.com*

7 Golfing Holidays
With more than 50 courses on the Costa del Sol *(see p103)* and ideal weather it's little wonder that the world comes here to play golf. Many hotels cater specifically to the golfer, and there are many specialist operators. ⊗ *Bill Goff Golfing Holidays, Unit 9, Bankside, The Watermark, Gateshead; 0870 401 2020*

8 Extreme Sports Tours
Scuba-diving, paragliding, hot-air ballooning, snowboarding – these are just a few of the more extreme sports you can find in Andalucía. ⊗ *Aviación del Sol, A376 km 114.5, Ronda; 952 87 72 49* • *Club Parapente Valle de Abdalajís, C/Sevilla 2, Valle de Abdalajís (Málaga); 952 48 91 80*

9 Sailing and Watersports
There are plenty of options for seafarers. ⊗ *Club de Mar de Almería, Playa de las Almadrabillas 1, Almería; 950 23 07 80* • *Real Club Mediterraneo de Málaga, Paseo de la Farola, Málaga; 952 22 63 00*

10 Pilgrimages
Andalucians take their religious pilgrimages seriously. If you want to join a *romería*, contact the local tourist board for exact dates, as all of them shift according to the lunar calendar or when weekends fall.

Left **Seville airport** Right **AVE high-speed trains in Seville**

🔟 Getting to Andalucía

1 By Air from Europe

Málaga is the main airport in Andalucía, but many other cities in the region also have airports – European flights also come into Seville, Jerez, Almería and Gibraltar. All airports have both bus and taxi services to city centres, except for Jerez, which only has taxis. ◈ *Air France: www.airfrance.fr • British Airways: www.british airways.com; UK 0870 850 9850; USA 800 247 9297 • Iberia: www.iberia.com; UK 0870 609 0500, USA 800 772 4642 • KLM: www.klm.com • Lufthansa: www. lufthansa.com*

2 By Air from outside Europe

Most international flights land at Málaga and the list of carriers is vast. The airport is 6 km (4 miles) southwest of the city. There is a train service to the east and west of the region, as well as buses. Taxis are also an option. ◈ *American Airlines, www. aa.com; USA 800 433 7300*

3 Charter & Budget Flights

Most air traffic to Andalucía is made up of charter flights, which are cheaper than scheduled flights. For budget flights to the region, try those recommended below:
◈ *www.easyjet.com*
• *www.ryanair.com*
• *www.vueling.com*

4 Packages

Most travel agencies will have slick, full-colour brochures touting these complete getaway deals, and the prices often include full- or half-board accommodation as well as transport. Be aware, however, that these packages are usually centred in the most congested and touristy resorts on the coast, and you may not get a true impression of Andalucía.

5 By Car

From Madrid, it is a day's drive down to Andalucía. To get to Spain with your own car from the UK, options include ferries to France or to the north of Spain itself. Another alternative is to load your car on to an overnight train from Paris and collect it in Madrid the next morning. ◈ *P&O European Ferries: 08705 980 333; www.poferries. com • Brittany Ferries: 8703 665 333; www.Brittany ferries.com • Motorail, SNCF France: 08448 48 40 50*

6 By Sea

The ferries from the UK connect with trains to Córdoba and Málaga direct from Bilbao, another with connections in Madrid from Santander. If you're coming to Andalucía from the Balearic Islands, there are ferries from Palma to Barcelona and Valencia, from which you can take the train down to the south.

7 By Bus

This option often works out to be more expensive than a low-cost flight. And from the UK, for example, it can be a gruelling 35-hour trip. Consider it as a last resort. ◈ *Eurolines: 080705 143219; www.eurolines.com*

8 By Train

From Madrid there are high-speed AVE trains daily to Seville and Málaga. The journey takes about 2 hours 30 minutes, with a stop in Córdoba. From Barcelona, the train trip to Seville (via Madrid) is about 5.5 hours. ◈ *RENFE: www.renfe.es*

9 Car Rentals

Renting a car in Andalucía is relatively cheap. Local firms will generally treat you better, even delivering and picking up the vehicle. Most companies require that drivers be at least 25 years old, with a valid licence and credit card. Make sure there are no hidden charges. ◈ *Hertz: www. hertz.com • Avis: www. avis.com • Europcar: www. europcar.com • Málaga companies: Autopro (also in Seville, Granada and Jerez): www.autopro.es; Dany Car: www.dany-car.com; Helle Hollis: www.hellehollis.com*

10 By Motorcycle

The same options as for cars apply for motorcycle travel. It's a great way to get around, especially for the hinterland.

Left **Seville bus station** Right **Taxis**

🔟 Getting Around Andalucía

1 By Bus
If you don't have your own wheels, the bus system is the best way to get around. Buses go to almost every village, sooner or later, and the roads have improved in recent years, shortening routes. There are dozens of companies dividing up the market. You can buy tickets on board. ✪ *Seville: Prado de San Sebastian, 954 41 71 11; Plaza de Armas, 954 90 80 40 • Granada: Ctra de Jaén, 958 18 54 80 • Córdoba: Glorieta de Tres Culturas s/n, 957 40 40 40 • Málaga: Paseo de los Tilos, 952 35 00 61*

2 By Train
Train connections between major towns are fairly developed and there are some regional routes as well. Stations in Seville, Córdoba and Málaga are efficient and user-friendly; however, expect many stops along the way. ✪ *Seville: Santa Justa, Avda Kansas City, 902 24 02 02 • Granada: Avda Andaluces, 902 24 02 02 • Córdoba: Glorieta de las Tres Culturas, 902 24 02 02 • Málaga: Explanada de la Estación, 902 24 02 02 • www.renfe.es*

3 By Metro
In 2009, a new subway system was introduced in Seville, providing a cost-effective and efficient means of transport for people based in the outer suburbs.

4 By Car
Many of the main roads in the region are less than 10 years old and in great condition. The problem is that, as a result, older maps can be confusingly out of date. Expect chaotic driving conditions, as locals pay little attention to rules and signs. Parking in towns and cities can be a real problem – leave the car in a car park and walk.

5 By Motorcycle
This is an excellent way to visit the out of the way areas and to discover a side of the region that most pass by. For steep inclines you'll need a good-sized bike, but if you're on the coast a scooter will do. Helmets are required by law.

6 Boating
With all the marinas up and down both coasts this mode of transport is a natural if you can afford it. But you'll need to be an experienced sailor to deal with the heavy currents that dominate the waters around the Strait of Gibraltar – for most, it's best to stick close to either coast. ✪ *Royal Spanish Sailing Federation: 915 19 50 08; www.rfev.es*

7 By Taxi
Taxis are an affordable way to get around towns – you can find plenty of them cruising the streets to be flagged down. Some have no meters, but the drivers are usually honest about how much the fare should be. It is customary to give the driver a small tip. ✪ *Seville: 954 58 00 00 • Granada: 958 28 06 54 • Córdoba: 957 76 44 44 • Malaga: 952 33 33 33*

8 By Bicycle
Cycling is a major sport all over Spain – especially here, where the weather is so conducive. You'll see enthusiasts on even the steepest mountain roads. In Seville, a city-hall operated bike rental scheme enables a more relaxed ride. ✪ *Spanish Cycling Federation: 915 40 08 41, www.rfec.com • www.carrilbicisevilla.es*

9 Hiking
This is the best way to explore mountainous areas, and there are many local organizations that are able to help you with maps, suggestions and advice. Make sure you have adequate gear, including cold weather or sun protection. ✪ *Federación Española de Deportes de Montaña, Granada: 958 29 13 40 • Nevadensis, C/Verónica, Pampaneira (Granada): 958 76 31 27*

10 Walking
This is the best way to take in Andalucía's cities and towns, mainly because every inch of their historic centres is worth a close look.

The heat in high summer can be crushing – always carry water, take a break during siesta time and wear a hat and sunscreen.

129

Left **Pavement peddlers** Right **Mountain road**

TOP 10 Things to Avoid

1 Illegal Budget Hotels

Some budget hotels, especially in Granada's Albaicín area, run a "bait and switch" scheme. Guests are welcomed at a pretty location only to be told that their room is housed in a different, much less charming, building. These places do not issue receipts and do not have a complaints book, both of which are requirements to operate legally.

2 Rancid Food

In the heat of the summer, it's wise to be attentive to the freshness of what you consume. Tapas (see pp70–71) that look as though they've been around a day too long, anything to do with mayonnaise that's been sitting out of the fridge and, of course, shellfish served in less than fastidiously hygienic establishments are probably best refused.

3 Religious Disrespect

Despite the casual dress code that predominates here, it is still a good idea to dress respectfully when you visit places of worship, and not to visit at all during mass or religious ceremonies.

4 Fakes & Forgeries

Be wary of supposed "originals". Copies, prints, forgeries and outright fakes do brisk business.

If you decide to buy any of these pieces, be very certain you're pledging your trust to a dealer whose credentials are beyond reproach – and get certificates of authentication and guarantees.

5 "Mystery" Tours

In the most heavily touristed zones you'll occasionally be offered a tour that, on the face of it, looks like something for nothing. It might be a daytrip to some interesting sight at a remarkably cut-rate price, or even an offer of cash or a lavish meal for just going to inspect a new condo or time-share project. These are not promotional bargains in the usual sense, but heavy-handed sales ploys and should be steered clear of.

6 Beach Snacks

Many of the snack bars you find along the beaches, especially the most popular beaches, are overpriced. If you want to hang out in such places to enjoy the people-watching, then just get a drink. For meals, head away from the waterfront and into the towns. Make sure the menu shows the prices, or you might get a shock with the bill.

7 Flower Girls

These women appear friendly enough when they flounce up to you and try to hand you a flower or a sprig of rose-

mary. But once you take the bait, they demand a lot of money for their cheery little "gift". Do your best to avoid them.

8 Peddlers

Most pavement peddlers will just call out to you a word or two about their merchandise, but once you evince an interest, you will be under pressure to buy something. Make it clear from the outset that you might want to look, but you'll decide what, if anything, you're going to buy. Check all merchandise thoroughly for defects, especially clothing, and then offer half the asking price.

9 Hair-raising Roads

Some mountain roads are narrow, winding and skirt yawning chasms. Most highways, however, have been widened and do not present any risks. Do watch out for aggressive drivers, though. Always stay in the right lane, except to overtake, and follow the rules of the road, as the police keep a close watch.

10 Street Scams

An age-old gambling con in busy pedestrian areas is the shell game. The main man shuffles three cups, showing you how easy it is to follow the one that covers the pea, or whatever. Don't be taken in – you'll never win a game.

In peak seasons, traffic jams in towns and on the coastal highway may present the biggest challenge to visitors.

Left **Quiet off-season beach** Right **Picnic area sign**

🔟 Budget Tips

1 Package Deals
If you choose carefully, making sure that you end up in a fairly pleasant part of the coast or near the sights you want to see, all-inclusive packages can be excellent value. They are particularly appealing if all you mainly want is to be handily situated for the beach and have most of your meals covered into the bargain.

2 Picnicking
Given the wealth of natural beauty here, much of it now given over to parks and reserves, there are excellent picnicking opportunities everywhere. There are also plenty of grocers for all that you'll need to put together a memorable repast, with settings and views thrown in. Be sure to pick up your litter afterwards.

3 Self-Catering
You'll certainly need to book very much in advance to secure one of the less expensive self-catering apartments. But it's worth it, not only for the money you'll save but also for the freedom you'll enjoy in doing the region entirely your own way *(see p146)*.

4 Partying
Some of the most happening bars and clubs are free to enter and require nothing of you but to have a good time. No cover charges or mini-mum charges is a reality here – most of the bars are so busy that no one will notice that you're nursing your brew all night long. Beer, wine and *tinto de verano* are the chepest options, while mixed drinks can be quite pricey.

5 Camping
There are some 130 authorized campsites in the region, mostly along the coast. Camping rough is legal, although not particularly encouraged. It's prohibited within 1 km (half a mile) of an official campsite, in urban areas, and in zones prohibited for military or ecological reasons. Get permission from the landowner first *(see p147)*.

6 IVA
If you buy anything that has a hefty sales tax tacked onto it and you are a non-EU citizen, keep the receipt, fill out the paperwork, then when you leave you can get a portion of it reimbursed at the airport. Another option for avoiding the 7 per cent IVA tax is to have your purchases shipped directly home.

7 Menú del Día
The daily lunch menu in most restaurants can save you a great deal – as much as 75 per cent of the regular *à la carte* cost. Portions are generally generous, too, so you can make this your major meal of the day. It's also a great way to savour the cuisine of some of the top restaurants without forking out over-the-top prices.

8 Laundromats
A few *lavanderías automáticas* can be found in cities, but don't bother looking anywhere else. Regular laundries and *tintorerías* (dry-cleaners) are quite expensive, and hotel services are even more exorbitant. Bring a packet of travel washing detergent with you.

9 Reduced Admissions
Coupons for reduced group admissions to various attractions can help a lot when you've got a whole family to pay for. You'll find them in various magazines, weekly papers, flyers, brochures and handed out on the street in busy areas. Tourist offices also often have stacks of them lying around as promotional lures.

10 Off-Season Travel
This is by far the best way to make your money go further. Prices plummet as the throngs of July and August become a faint memory. Low-season prices for everything can delight the budget-minded traveller, plus you have the luxury of being one of only a few, rather than amid vast hordes.

Left **ATM machine** Centre **Logo of the Spanish telecom system** Right **Postbox**

🔟 Banking and Communications

1 Currency
Now that the euro is the currency of many European countries, life is much easier for visitors to the continent, although the changeover has resulted in some price inflation. Euro bank-notes have the following denominations: 5, 10, 20, 50, 100, 200 and 500. Euro coins come in eight denominations: €1, €2, and 1, 2, 5, 10, 20 and 50 cents. Visitors from out-side the euro zone should check the exchange rates at the time of travel.

2 Traveller's Cheques
If you're going to opt for this safety precaution, get your cheques directly in euros – you won't have to pay any commission to cash them and, in some places, you'll be able to use them as cash. Make sure you keep track of the serial numbers.

3 Cashpoints and ATMs
For ready cash, this is the best option. Bank machines are every-where and very reliable. Spanish banks charge no transaction fee; you'll only have your own bank's fee to pay for using a non-branch machine.

4 Credit Cards
Using your credit card is possible for almost everything in larger towns. Only the smallest places in off-the-beaten-track outposts will find it a problem. However, be aware that your own bank may charge you a 2 per cent currency con-version fee for every card purchase you make, so it's cheaper to use your cash card option.

5 Wiring Money
This expensive, laborious process should be considered only as a last resort. You can have your bank send money to a bank in Spain, but you must organize things at the Spanish end first. Then expect it to take an indeterminate number of days and for there to be substantial charges at both ends of the process.

6 Post
Post offices *(correos)* are open 9am to 2pm and 5pm to 7:30pm, although larger offices do not close for siesta. For letters and postcards, you can also get stamps *(sellos)* at tobacco shops and news-paper stands. In general, Spanish post is reliable.

7 Telephones
Calling Spain from another country requires dialling 00 then the country code, 34. While in Andalucía, you must always dial the regional area code, 95, even if call-ing locally. To call abroad from Spain, dial 00, then the country code, area code and number of your destination. For local and national information, call 11850; for international enquiries, call 11825.

8 Internet
Many hotels now allow you to use your laptop for accessing the Internet. Internet cafés are also common sights in every town and city, and even villages. Wi-Fi is quite common too, but it can be expensive and the connection may not be completely reliable.

9 Newspapers and Magazines
In the larger towns, you'll find a good selection of international press: *USA Today* and the *Inter-national Herald Tribune* are available in the larger kiosks, as well as major British, German, French and Dutch papers. Costa del Sol English-language magazines include *The Entertainers*, *Lookout* and *Marbella Life*.

10 TV and Radio
The more expensive hotels all offer satellite TV, with many programm-es in English, German, French and Italian – not to mention all the regular Spanish channels. Radio Gibraltar and US Armed Forces Radio from Rota provide English-language broadcasting, and there are others along the Costa del Sol. Spanish stations feature a mix of Spanish and international pop music. Canal Sur is the official Andalucían broadcasting system.

Mobile phones work well all over Andalucía but check with your network whether you are set up for international usage.

Left **Police car** Right **Pharmacy sign**

🔟 Security and Health

1 Precautions
There are no special inoculations required to visit Andalucía. The only protection you should be sure to use on a regular basis is sunscreen – sunburn and heat stroke are the main sources of discomfort. Some people also experience a slight upset stomach from the change in bacteria in the food and water, although tap water is safe to drink.

2 Prescriptions
If there are any prescription medicines you require, or may require, it's best to bring them along with you. Due to differing pharmaceutical regulations, different countries may or may not have the drugs you need, or they may be sold under a different name.

3 Emergencies
For any emergency, give precise information about what is needed and where exactly you are, in Spanish if you are able.

4 Pharmacies
Pharmacies *(farmacias)* are a good source of medical advice for minor complaints. The pharmacists are highly trained, often speak good English, and may be able to sell medicines that would normally only be available by prescription at home. In major towns you'll find at least one pharmacy open 24 hours.

5 Multilingual Doctors
If you are seriously ill and need a doctor who speaks your language, you can get details from your local consulate *(see p126)*, hotel, pharmacy or tourist office. If you need someone who works under the EU health plan, make sure that the doctor is part of the Spanish health care system; otherwise, be prepared to pay and be reimbursed later by your insurance company.

6 Disabled Travellers
Generally speaking, Andalucía is not very well set up for travellers with any sort of disability. The best bet for adequate facilities are the newer hotels, since the law requires that all new public buildings be fully accessible. Older structures will present problems for those in wheelchairs *(see p134)*.

7 Condoms
Condoms need no longer be smuggled into Spain, as they had to be during the Franco era.

Emergency Numbers

Any Emergency: *112*
Fire: *080*
Ambulance: *061*
National Police: *091*
Civil Guard: *062*
Local Police: *092*

They are available in pharmacies, bars and even vending machines on the street.

8 Accidents
In the case of an accident dial the emergency number or call the *Cruz Roja* (Red Cross), who will send an ambulance and paramedics. There are good international hospitals along the Costa del Sol, and in major cities.
Ⓢ *Red Cross: Hospital Victoria Eugenia; Avda de la Cruz Roja; Seville; 954 35 14 00 • Hospital Costa del Sol: Ctra Nacional 340 km 187; Marbella, 952 76 98 50 • Hospital Virgen de las Nieves: Avda de las Fuerzas Armadas, Granada; 958 02 00 00 • Hospital Reina Sofía: Avda Menéndez Pidal, Córdoba, 957 01 00 00*

9 Petty Crime
In any crowded area, there are bound to be pickpockets. The best solution is not to carry any valuables in easily accessible places. Wallets should be safely tucked into inside closed pockets or under your clothing in a money belt. Never leave bags unattended.

10 Serious Crime
Serious crime is virtually unheard of in this pleasure-loving land. Naturally, however, it's wise not to wander down a deserted, unlit alley at night, especially in the seedier quarters.

Left **Disabled sign** Centre **Students in Andalucía** Right **Public convenience sign**

🔟 Special Concerns

1 Disabled Travellers

Historically lagging behind in providing for people with mobility problems, Spain has begun to catch up in recent years. At least at the airport you should find adequate facilities – as long as you notify your travel agent and/or airline of your needs in advance and then reconfirm a week before departure.

2 Disabled Accommodation

The older buildings, often refurbished medieval structures, are usually entirely without facilities for the disabled – there are endless stairways and levels to contend with, sometimes even within a single room. Stay in the newest hotel you can find, where lifts and bathrooms will probably be large enough and will all comply with EU laws. But check details before booking.
🕓 *Access-Able Travel Services: www.access-able.com • All Go Here: www.allgohere.com • Access Travel: 01942 888844; www.access-travel.co.uk • Mobility International USA, Eugene, OR; (541) 343-1284, www.miusa.org • Australian National Disability Services: 02 628 33200, www.nds.org.au • Organización Nacional de Ciegos de España (ONCE): C/Resolana 30, Seville; 954 90 16 16; www.once.es*

3 Senior Citizens

The area is very senior-friendly, given the large numbers of inter-national retirees who choose these sunny climes. Many apartment complexes are designed exclusively with seniors in mind, and hotels as well. Seniors also qualify for discounted fees to many sights, travel and even some hotels.

4 Resources for Seniors

There are several educational organizations that cater to seniors, with extensive residential cultural programmes of all types. In addition, the Junta de Andalucía has a helpline for those who can speak Spanish.
🕓 *Senior Helpline: 900 22 22 23 • Elderhostel: www. elderhostel.org*

5 Women Travellers

Compared to Northern Europe, attitudes here towards women can be pretty macho. Still, women generally do not encounter harassment and can travel alone with-out a problem. Naturally, exercise normal care, especially after dark.

6 Helplines

The Junta de Andalucía runs several helplines, which are free calls from any phone, but they are Spanish-speaking only. 🕓 *Women: 900 20 09 99 • Drug addiction: 900 84 50 40*

7 Student Travellers

Many students come to study in Seville, Granada and Córdoba. With a valid International Student ID Card, you're entitled to some price reductions on entrance fees and travel. There are student information centres in major cities.
🕓 *Instituto Andaluz de la Juventud: C/O'Donnell 22, Seville; 955 03 63 50 • Centro Municipal de Información Juvenil: C/Veronica de la Magdalena 23, Granada; 958 22 20 53 • La Casa de la Juventud: C/Campo Madre de Dios, Córdoba; 957 76 47 07*

8 Public Conveniences

Public toilets are scarce, but bars are everywhere and they are legally bound to let you use their facilities. An "S" on the door stands for *Señoras* (Ladies) and a "C" indicates *Caballeros* (Gents), although there are variations.

9 Gay Travellers

In more cosmopolitan areas, attitudes towards gays and lesbians are relaxed, but less so in rural areas. 🕓 *Asociación Andaluza de Lesbianas y Gays: Granada, 958 20 06 02; www.acosiacionnos.org*

10 Gay Areas

Torremolinos is gay-central for nightlife *(see p104)*. Seville, Granada and Cádiz also have sig-nificant gay populations.

Note that many Spanish bars do not have toilet paper, so it is worth carrying some tissues on you.

Left **Andalucían theme park** Right **Family on the beach**

Tips for Families

1 Accommodation Breaks

Most accommodation options here – unless they specifically request "adults only" – truly welcome families. Hotels often allow you to include any children up to a certain age – sometimes as high as the teens – at no extra charge, except perhaps a nominal fee for the extra bed or two. The best option for most families is a self-catered apartment *(see p146)*.

2 Meals for Kids

Most restaurants have special kids' meals, and some even have separate menus with things that will please children's palates. Many will also prepare special foods for infants. There are also fast-food restaurants that cater to kids' tastes.

3 Shopping for Kids

There are shops galore that focus on what kids want, from toys to beach gear to clothes and gadgets. Most of the stuff is cheap – and cheaply made – so you can stock up on what they need without worrying about the budget.

4 Sights for Kids

Some of the theme parks and museums have exhibits and activities, as well as special playgrounds, that are designed entirely with children in mind. Andalucía's caves, too, are a big hit with youngsters, instilling them with a rich awareness of the wonders of nature.

5 Kids' Activities

Besides the sea, the region also has a number of commercial waterparks and amusement parks, replete with slides and other facilities for children to burn up a full-day's energy. It's healthy, outdoor fun that the whole family can participate in.

6 Teenagers

Teenagers of every nationality quickly fall in with each other soon after arrival in the most touristed areas, establishing a routine of beaching it during the day and going out at night. There's plenty of high-energy action to get up to while the sun shines. When the sun goes down, it's time to prepare for the forthcoming social whirl.

7 Nightlife

In the very touristy resorts, which depend on families for much of their trade, many clubs will allow entrance for older teens, although the minimum legal age for drinking is 18. Depending on what curfew, if any, is imposed by parental authority, the dancing can go on till dawn. The Spanish in general are very relaxed about the presence of children in bars and pubs.

8 Hotel Offerings

Many of the larger hotels and resorts have a full programme of activities for guests of every age. These may include water aerobics, water polo, or other exercise regimes – or anything from crafts classes for adults to organized games for pre-schoolers. Most such activities are scheduled on a weekly basis, with a monthly calendar posted in some conspicuous spot in the foyer.

9 Babysitting

Some hotels also offer babysitting services, especially those that cater primarily to package tourists. The cost of this service may be included in the package, so confirm that it is, if such an option exists. Other hotels may have a play area, supervised by qualified personnel.

10 Transport Options

The best option when you have small children is not to move around much – the kids will be able to adjust and enjoy themselves more readily. Children under four travel free on trains; ages four to eleven pay 60 percent of the fare. Entry fees are either reduced or free to many sights and museums.

Left **Outside dining in Andalucía** Right **Seafood**

⏱10 Eating and Drinking Tips

1 Eating Out
Both lunch and dinner hours tend to be late in Spain. Lunchtime is no earlier than 1:30pm, and even 3pm is perfectly normal. Dinner is usually no earlier than 9pm, and sitting down at a table as late as 11pm is not unheard of. A reservation is never a bad idea, and smart-casual dress is perfectly fine at most establishments.

2 Breakfast
Breakfast in Andalucía is generally coffee and *tostada* (toast); the latter may be drizzled with olive oil and can also be topped with crushed tomatoes, ham or *manteca colorá* (pork lard with paprika). Only foreign-run venues offer a full English or American breakfast. Many hotels cater to international taste with a buffet spread.

3 Tapas and Raciones
Tapas (see pp68–9) are a Spanish institution and nowhere more prevalent than here. Locals eat them as appetizers before heading off to dinner, but a few well-chosen *tapas* can easily make a full meal. *Raciones* are larger portions of the same dishes.

4 Menú del Día
Many places offer a *menú del día* (daily menu) at lunchtime, which usually means considerable savings compared to *à la carte* prices. You get a very limited choice of a first course (typically soup or salad) and second course (fish or meat, with side orders) and dessert, with water and wine included. Coffee is usually extra, or in place of dessert.

5 Meats
Pork in all its guises is the central meat in the Andalucían diet, with Jabugo mountain-cured ham considered the crowning glory. Duck, rabbit, quail and other game are also quite common, with beef and veal present but not so important. Chicken is very common, and goat and lamb are also featured on many menus all over the region.

6 Seafood
Even along the crowded Costa del Sol, the few remaining fishermen still manage to haul in the full bounty that the Mediterranean has to offer. And the abundance from the Atlantic coast is even more impressive. A local speciality is *rape* (monkfish), and various types of crustacean and shellfish include lobster, crayfish, prawns and mussels *(see pp66–7)*.

7 Side Dishes and Dessert
Favourite side dishes include *papas fritas* (chips), asparagus, both green and white, and mushrooms sautéed with garlic, as well as whatever vegetables may be in season. Fresh fruit is always an option for dessert, along with a range of baked treats and several types of custard.

8 Drinks
Wine and beer are the top choices, usually accompanied by a small bottle of mineral water, either still or sparkling. Sangría is prevalent, too, but the regional drink of choice is *vino de Jerez* (sherry), or one of the sweet wines from Málaga. Coffee can be with or without milk and you can also ask for it *descafeinado* (decaffeinated) *(see p67)*.

9 Vegetarian and Vegan Options
Such choices are few and far between on most menus around the region. Meat is used in almost everything, and even the vegetable dishes are usually enhanced with a bit of pork. One good recourse would be to have the chef make a salad for you, leaving out any non-vegetarian ingredients. Or head for one of the few vegetarian restaurants.

10 Tipping
Although tipping is not an absolute necessity here, it is customary to leave about 10 per cent of the total bill, or at least to round the figure up.

Left **Typical mountain hotel bedroom** Right **Hotel grading sign**

🔟 Accommodation Tips

1 Where to Stay

This extensive region offers a tremendous range of climes and terrains, from sophisticated city life, to mountains, to subtropical beaches, to wild, open plains. If you have the time, sample a bit of all of these, each of them beautiful and satisfying.

2 Accommodation Types

Determining your needs and desires before you book will ensure a happier stay. Andalucía has a vast range of accommodation options, from resorts (see p142), government-run paradors, often in historic buildings (see p140), converted farmhouses (see p145), to camping and hostels (see p147). If you want to see many of the region's sights but only want one base, consider renting a car.

3 Choosing the Best Base

Decide first how much of the region you want to see, and how much time you want to spend in differing terrains. Then choose whether to be based in a bustling area, in a smaller village, or in a more remote location. Options exist right on the sea, up in the mountains, or on private *fincas* (ranches), either working farms or those that have been transformed into pleasant resorts.

4 Price Considerations

The range of accommodation costs is very wide. You can get pretty much whatever you want in terms of location by spending very little. Andalucía tends to be less expensive than many other destinations of equal or greater quality.

5 Making Reservations

If you plan to visit in high season make reservations as far in advance as possible. The good-value accommodations fill up quickly and even high-end gems can be booked solid in the months of July and August. You will need a credit card number with expiry date to book, and you should confirm every detail – exact dates, type of accommodation, number of beds – with the hotel management by sending an e-mail and/or a fax.

6 Finding Something on the Spot

Unless you want to face hours of casting about for a room and possibly not finding anything in your price range, this practice is not recommended here, except in low season when you can, indeed, find plenty of options and good prices. Do be aware, however, that many establishments close for up to several months during the winter.

7 Tipping

Tipping in Spain, as in many countries in Europe, is not absolutely necessary. Workers are paid living wages and do not depend on your tips. However, a few coins for services rendered by the hotel staff are never amiss. You can tip porters and bellboys on the spot, and leave something for the maid in your room.

8 Hidden Extras

A tax of 7 per cent may or may not be included in the quoted price of your accommodation. Parking, phone use and breakfast also may or may not be charged as extra, so determine what you are liable for in advance.

9 Travelling with Children

Andalucía is well set up for family travel. With very few exceptions, children are welcome at every hotel or resort, and those under certain ages may even stay free, with no extra charge for roll-away beds or cots. Many hotels have a schedule of events with kids in mind, often at no extra charge.

10 Language

With so many years of tourism, many Andalucians are multi-lingual. However, it's a good idea to learn a little Spanish, at least for getting around the more rural areas.

There are no official tourist agencies that handle hotel reservations in Andalucía.

Left **Hotel Alfonso XIII** Right **Hotel Casa Imperial**

Seville Stays

1 Hotel Alfonso XIII
This historic palace, erected by the eponymous king to house royals and other dignitaries during the 1929 Exposition, is suitably sumptuous. Unfortunately, it's now part of a US chain, whose management just doesn't seem as *au fait* with the subtleties of European-style luxury. The hotel is undergoing a refurbishment that is due to be completed by 2011; it remains open during this time. ✆ *C/San Fernando 2 • Map M4 • 954 91 70 00 • www. alfonsoxiii.com • €€€€€*

2 Hotel Casa Imperial
This luxurious choice in the Barrío de Santa Cruz provides a memorable stay. It's a converted 16th-century palace, set among a series of patios. Many rooms have sunken baths and all are uniquely decorated in the very finest taste, loaded with antiques. Included is the use of a nearby gym and pool. ✆ *C/Imperial 29 • Map N2 • 954 50 03 00 • www. casaimperial.com • €€€€€*

3 Hotel Taberna del Alabardero
Seven elegant rooms are gathered around a central patio filled with greenery and light. The restaurant boasts a Michelin star. ✆ *C/Zaragoza 20 • Map L3 • 954 50 27 21 • www. tabernadelalabardero.es • Closed Aug • €€€*

4 Melía Colón Hotel
This grand five-star hotel offers its guests traditional Andalucían elegance and maximum comfort. Enjoy fabulous views from the solarium, cool off in the pool or relax in the spa. ✆ *C/ Canalejas 1 • Map L2 • 954 50 55 99 • www. solmelia.com • €€€€€*

5 EME fusionhotel
One of Seville's most talked-about hotels, this place stands out as much for its central location, opposite the cathedral, as for its avant-garde decor and trendy ambience. Highlights include a spa, Japanese-style eatery, lively *tapas* bar and a stunning rooftop lounge with unparalleled views. ✆ *C/Alemanes 27 • Map M3 • 954 56 00 00 • www. emehotel.com • €€€€€*

6 Hotel Vime Corregidor
Located just around the corner from the lively Alameda de Hercules, in a bohemian part of town, this hotel is comfortable, clean and convenient. ✆ *C/Morgado 17 • Map M1 • 954 38 51 11 • www.vime hoteles.com • €€*

7 Alcoba del Rey
The decor is Indian and Moroccan in style and rooms feature king-size canopy beds. The rooftop terrace has great views. ✆ *C/Becquer 9 • Map N1 • 954 91 58 00 • www. alcobadelrey.com • €€€€€*

8 Las Casas del Rey de Baeza
Close to La Casa de Pilatos, this chic hotel is located in a beautiful setting, which fuses historic traditional architecture with modern style. The shaded walkways and stone flooring are completed by natural tones in the courtyards. The rooftop pool is a bonus in summer. ✆ *Plaza Jesús de la Redención 2 • Map N2 • 954 56 14 96 • www.hospes.es • €€€€€*

9 Hostals Picasso, Van Gogh & Dali
These three cheery *pensions*, under the same management, are well located between the cathedral and the alcázar. Potted plants give the places an inviting feel and rooms are clean and comfortable. ✆ *Hostal Picasso: C/San Gregorio 1; Map M4; € • Hostal Van Gogh: C/Miguel Mañara 4; Map M4; 954 56 37 27; €€ • Hostal Dali: C/Puerta Jerez 3; 954 22 95 05; €*

10 Olé Backpacker
Centrally located in the Arenal district, this hostel provides budget accommodation in a clean and well-maintained setting. Facilities include free Wi-Fi, air con, a TV room and bikes for rent. Shared baths. ✆ *C/Santas Patronatas 31 • Map L3 • 954 22 21 32 • www. olebackpacker.com • €*

Note: *Unless otherwise stated, all hotels accept credit cards, have en-suite bathrooms and air conditioning*

Price Categories

For a standard, double room per night (with breakfast if included), taxes and extra charges.

€	under €50
€€	€50–€100
€€€	€100–€150
€€€€	€150–€200
€€€€€	over €200

Above **Alhambra Palace**

TOP 10 Granada Sojourns

1 Parador de San Francisco

You'll need to book about a year in advance to stay here, but it's the premier stay in town. Housed in a meticulously restored 15th-century monastery, with a wisteria-covered patio, it is utterly beautiful. For the maximum experience, get a room with a view out over the Albaicín on one side and the cloister on the other. 🌐 *C/Real de la Alhambra • Map R2 • 958 22 14 40 • www.parador.es • €€€€€*

2 Alhambra Palace

The style of this *belle époque* extravaganza is neo-Moorish. Located just steps away from the Nasrid palace, it offers great views from every room, terrace and balcony. The public rooms are palatial. 🌐 *C/Peña Partida 2–4 • Map R3 • 958 22 14 68 • www.h-alhambrapalace.es • €€€€*

3 Roommate Migueletes

This meticulously restored 13th-century mansion is just steps from Plaza Nueva. A charming hotel, it has just 23 rooms and two suites and is a romantic retreat in the heart of the Albaicín. The interior is decorated with Moroccan antiques and rooms look onto the interior courtyard or out to the Alhambra. 🌐 *C/Benalúa 11 • Map R2 • 958 21 07 00 • www.casamigueletes.com • €€€*

4 El Ladrón de Agua

This enchanting boutique hotel is situated in a 16th-century mansion in a superb location. Eight of the beautifully but simply decorated rooms have views of the Alhambra. A sumptuous retreat. 🌐 *Carrera del Darro • Map R2 • 958 21 50 40 • www.ladrondeagua.com • €€€*

5 Hotel Reina Cristina

Everything has been kept more or less the same as when the poet Garcia Lorca was forced to hide out here – this is the last place the poet stayed, before his untimely end *(see p57)*. Each room has unique style and there are patios and fountains in the public areas. 🌐 *C/Tablas 4 • Map F4 • 958 25 32 11 • www.hotelreinacristina.com • €€€*

6 Posada Pilar del Toro

Another charming hotel in the heart of the Albaicín. This *posada* features traditional wooden beams and ceramic tiles, creating a rustic ambience with modern comforts. 🌐 *C/Elvira 25 • Map Q2 • 958 22 73 33 • www.posadadeltoro.com • €€*

7 Cuevas El Abanico

In this self-catering "cave" hotel, the whitewashed interiors are immaculate and loaded with rustic charm. No need for air conditioning – you have an entire hill of earth overhead to keep out the heat. A picturesque and uniquely Andalucían choice. Minimum two-night stay. 🌐 *Verea de Enmedio • Map F4 • 958 22 61 99 • www.el-abanico.com • €€*

8 Hostal Suecia

In a leafy cul-de-sac, this is every inch a traditional Spanish house, with terracotta tiles, arched windows and a large patio. The rooftop terrace is perfect for admiring the nearby Alhambra. 🌐 *C/Molinos (Huerta de los Angeles) 8 • Map R3 • 958 22 50 44 • No air conditioning • €*

9 Hotel Zaguan del Darro

A former Franciscan convent, this 16th-century palace has been restored to retain its original style. Rooms are charming, and several have outstanding views. 🌐 *Carrera del Darro 23 • Map R2 • 958 21 57 30 • www.hotelzaguan.com • €€*

10 Instalación Juvenil Granada

This youth hostel is clean, although it is quite far away from the city centre. Its advantage, however, is that there are only two or three to a room, and the bathrooms are all en-suite. 🌐 *C/Ramón y Cajal 2 • Map F4 • 958 00 29 00 • www.inturjoven.com • Dis. access • No credit cards • €*

 Granada's historic centre has restricted vehicle access limited to residents and hotel guests. Call your hotel to gain entry.

Left **Parador de Ronda** Right **Parador Arcos de la Frontera**

Paradors

1 Parador de Ayamonte

At the mouth of the River Guadiana, this modern facility features sunlit rooms and a perfect position for exploring the area where Huelva Province meets Portugal. Most rooms afford panoramic views of the Atlantic from the high point of town. Local cuisine emphasizes fish, such as ray and monkfish, as well as rural dishes. ○ *Avda de la Constitucíon s/n • Map A4 • 959 32 07 00 • Dis. access • €€€*

2 Parador de Mazagón

Unspoiled beauty on the shores of the sea is what this modern property is all about. It's ideal for those who want to commune with nature, especially with the wonders of the Coto Doñana, nearby. Facilities include gardens, pools and a sauna – all facing on to Mazagón beach. Seafood and Iberian ham are culinary specialities. ○ *Playa de Mazagón • Map B4 • 959 53 63 00 • Dis. access • €€€€*

3 Parador de Mójacar

This beachside parador, 1.5 km (1 mile) from the village of Mójacar and 3 km (1.8 miles) from a golf course, has an inviting atmosphere with spectacular views from the bedroom terraces and the upstairs dining room. Ultra-modern, clean and child-friendly. ○ *Paseo del Mediterraneo 339 • Map H4 • 950 47 82 50 • Dis. access • €€€*

4 Parador Arcos de la Frontera

Located on the banks of the Río Guadalete, this parador has an impressive view of the fertile plain of the river and of the old part of town. An ideal starting point for the *pueblos blancos* routes, as well as Jerez de la Frontera. The courtyard is graced with traditional latticework and ceramic tiles. ○ *Plaza del Cabildo • Map C5 • 956 70 05 00 • Dis. access • €€€€*

5 Parador Alcázar del Rey, Carmona

One of the most impressive of all the paradors, this is a 14th-century Moorish fortress-palace overlooking the Río Corbones. Rooms are large and decorated in classic Andalucían style, set off by antiques. Charming touches include a garden pool and expansive terrace. ○ *Alcázar • Map C3 • 954 14 10 10 • €€€€*

6 Parador de Ronda

One of the best sites in this evocative hill town. Set in the former town hall, views from the rooms are amazing, while the decor reflects the colours of the area. ○ *Plaza de España • Map D5 • 952 87 75 00 • €€€€*

7 Parador de Antequera

This quiet parador, surrounded by gardens and a swimming pool, is near the spectacular El Torcal (see p99). ○ *García del Olmo • Map D4 • 952 84 02 61 • Dis. access • €€€*

8 Parador del Gilbralfaro, Málaga

This parador stands surrounded by pine trees, facing the Alcázaba. It's handy for activities, notably golf and tennis, nearby. ○ *Castillo de Gibralfaro • Map S4 • 952 22 19 02 • Dis. access • €€€€*

9 Parador Castillo de Santa Catalina, Jaén

The superb location of this castle once made it the defensive bastion of Jaén. Inside, high crossed arches in the living and dining rooms show a marked Arabic character, and the comfortable bedrooms enjoy panoramic views. ○ *Map E3 • 953 23 00 00 • €€€€*

10 Parador Condestable Dávalos, Úbeda

Live like 16th-century nobility in this Renaissance palace, in the heart of one of Spain's most remarkably preserved historic centres. Rooms reflect the noble tone, with high ceilings and antique furnishings. ○ *Plaza de Vázquez Molina • Map F2 • 953 75 03 45 • €€€€*

For more information on paradors in Andalucía, visit the website www.parador.es

Price Categories

For a standard, double room per night (with breakfast if included), taxes and extra charges.

€ under €50
€€ €50–€100
€€€ €100–€150
€€€€ €150–€200
€€€€€ over €200

Above **Club Maritimo de Sotogrande**

🔟 Luxury Hotels

Hotel Jerez, Jerez
All rooms have been decorated in a warm and comfortable style, with views of the tropical gardens and a large pool. Rooms have satellite TV and Internet connection. Many also have a Jacuzzi. ◎ *Avda Álvaro Domecq 35 • Map B5 • 956 30 06 00 • www.jerezhotel.com • Dis. access • €€€*

Hacienda la Boticaria, Alcalá de Guadiara
This elegant hotel is located outside of Seville in stunning grounds that feature a lake, large courtyards and lush gardens. A five-star resort, it boasts indoor and outdoor pools, spa, golf course and gym. ◎ *Ctra Alcalá-Utrera km 2 • Map C4 • 955 69 88 20 • www.la boticaria-hotel.com • €€€€€*

Club Maritimo de Sotogrande
This hotel is luxurious and tastefully decorated in neutral tones. There are amazing views from every room – sometimes even from the bathtub. Free bike use and discounts for golfing. ◎ *Puerto Deportivo, Sotogrande • Map C6 • 956 79 02 00 • www.slh.com/maritimo • Dis. access • €€€€*

Hotel Casa de Carmona
Welcome to over 400 years of luxury. With unparalleled style and tranquillity, this 16th-century palace has been lovingly converted into a hotel, joined to the exclusive *Relais & Châteaux* chain. Patios with lush plantings and the soothing sound of fountains, grand drawing rooms and exquisite decor create an opulent atmosphere. ◎ *Plaza de Lasso 1 • Map C3 • 954 19 10 00 • www.casadecarmona.com • Dis. access • €€€€*

El Juncal, Ronda
An old Spanish farm has been brilliantly converted. The 11 rooms, most with private terrace, are spacious and refined. Other touches include a pool with a beach, Jacuzzi and sauna, set amid gardens. ◎ *Ctra Ronda-El Burgo km1 • Map D5 • 952 16 11 70 • www.eljuncal.com • Dis. access • €€€€*

El Fuerte, Marbella
In the centre of Marbella, next to the sea and surrounded by subtropical gardens. Within easy walking distance of the historic quarter too, so that you can discover the "real" Marbella, as well as soak up the glamour. ◎ *Avda El Fuerte • Map D5 • 952 92 00 00 • www.fuertehoteles.com • Dis. access • €€€€*

Hotel-Casino Torrequebrada, Benalmádena
This deluxe, Vegas-style establishment also has a casino. All the rooms have a balcony with sea views. Recreation options include a pool, sauna, gym and tennis court. ◎ *Avda del Sol • Map D5 • 952 44 60 00 • www.torrequebrada.com • Dis. access • €€€€*

Hospes Palacio del Baílio, Córdoba
Dating back to the 16th century, this chic hotel is a complex of former granaries, coach houses and stables surrounded by beautiful, scented gardens and patios. ◎ *Ramirez de las Casas Deza 10–12 • Map D3 • 957 49 89 93 • www.hospes.es • Dis. access • €€€€€*

Husa Palacio de Mengibar
This artistically restored stately palace serves haute cuisine in the rustic restaurant housed in the old stables. Rooms are individually decorated and there is a lovely courtyard. ◎ *Plaza Constitución 8 • Map E2 • 953 37 40 43 • www.palaciodemengibar.com • Dis. access • €€€*

Gran Hotel Almería, Almería
Although this is an undistinguished highrise to look at, its rooms enjoy a balcony with a view of the sea. Only steps from the beach. ◎ *Avda Reina Regente 8 • Map G4 • 950 23 80 11 • www.almeriagranhotel.com • Dis. access • €€€*

Note: *Unless otherwise stated, all hotels accept credit cards, have en-suite bathrooms and air conditioning*

Left **View from the Hotel Paraíso del Mar** Right **Hotel La Fuente de la Higuera**

Resorts

1 Hotel Riu Atlántico, Huelva

A vast resort offering every facility you can think of amid its landscaped gardens and Mediterranean splendours, including several swimming pools, one for children, and a spa. ◈ *Punta del Moral s/n • Map A4 • 959 62 10 00 • www.riu.com • Dis. access • €€€*

2 Barcelo, Jerez

This hotel towers like a castle of pale yellow stucco beside one of Europe's top golf courses. Expect top service and lots of activity options. There are several restaurants and snack bars to choose from. ◈ *Ctra Jerez-Arcos km 9.6 • Map B5 • 956 15 12 00 • www.barcelojerez.com • Dis. access • €€€€*

3 Hotel Playa de la Luz, Rota

This hotel is set on an unspoiled beach nestled between pine forests and sand dunes. Most rooms have a terrace or balcony, and there are three restaurants and two bars. ◈ *Avda de la Diputación • Map B5 • 956 21 05 00 • www.hotelplayadelaluz.com • Dis. access • €€€*

4 Hotel Fuerte Conil, Conil de la Frontera

This resort is an award-winner, in recognition of its environmentally friendly practices. Located right on the beach, it's done up in Neo-Moorish style and is not far from the fishing village of Conil. Most rooms have balconies and sea views. There's a choice of restaurants, a pool, spa treatments and sports facilities. ◈ *Playa de la Fontanilla • Map B5 • 956 44 33 44 • www. fuertehoteles.com • Closed Nov–Feb • Dis. access • €€€*

5 Kempinski Resort Hotel, Estepona

One of the "Leading Hotels of the World", this place is nothing short of magnificent. The style is a whimsical take on Moorish and regional architecture that suits the seaside setting perfectly. ◈ *Ctra de Cádiz km 159 • Map D5 • 952 80 95 00 • www.kempinski-spain.com • €€€€€*

6 Marbella Club Hotel, Marbella

Another of the "Leading Hotels of the World", the beachfront rooms and suites harmonize with Andalucían-style villas enjoying private gardens and some with private pools. ◈ *Bulevar Príncipe Alfonso von Hoenlome • Map D5 • 952 82 22 11 • www.marbellaclub.com • €€€€€*

7 Hotel La Fuente de la Higuera, Ronda

In a renovated olive oil mill, traditional Spanish architecture has met post modern design. Individually designed interiors are detailed down to the last bathroom fitting. All rooms have a garden or terrace. ◈ *Partido de los Frontones • Map D5 • 952 11 43 55 • www.hotella fuente.com • Dis. access • €€€*

8 Hotel Vincci Rumaykiyya, Sierra Nevada, Monachil, Granada

With beautiful alpine decor and wonderful interior design this hotel is both spacious and luxurious. At the heart of this ski resort, the hotel has a chair lift service at its door. ◈ *Map F4 • 958 48 25 08 • www.vincci hoteles.com • Closed May–Nov • €€€€€*

9 Hotel Paraíso del Mar, Nerja

This hotel enjoys a view of the coast. Rooms facing the mountains are generally larger or with a Jacuzzi to compensate. ◈ *C/Prolongación de Carabeo 22 • Map E5 • 952 52 16 21 • www.hotel paraisodelmar.com • €€€*

10 Finca La Bobadilla, Granada Province

A fabulous resort, reminiscent of a tiny Moorish village with its own chapel. It is interlaced with gardens and patios. ◈ *exit 175 from A92 • Map E4 • 958 32 18 61 • www.barcelolabobadilla. com • €€€€€*

Note: *Unless otherwise stated, all hotels accept credit cards, have en-suite bathrooms and air conditioning*

Above **El Castillo**

Price Categories

For a standard, double room per night (with breakfast if included), taxes and extra charges.

€	under €50
€€	€50–€100
€€€	€100–€150
€€€€	€150–€200
€€€€€	over €200

 Historic Finds

1 El Cortijo de los Mimbrales, El Rocío

Grouped around flower-decked patios, this converted farm is a series of comfortable cottages that retain an authentic flavour. Private balconies and gardens grace many of the accommodations, and all around there are orange trees, bougainvillea, wisteria and jasmine perfuming the air. ✆ Ctra Rocío-Matalascañas A483 km 30 • Map B4 • 959 44 22 37 • www.cortijomimbrales.com • Dis. access • €€€

2 Monasterio San Miguel, El Puerto de Santa María

This former monastery with Baroque architecture and art is nevertheless up-to-date with the luxuries it offers. Facilities include an excellent restaurant, pool, gardens and a solarium. ✆ C/Virgen de los Milagros 27 • Map B5 • 956 54 04 40 • www.jale.com/monasterio • Dis. access • €€€

3 La Casa Noble, Aracena

This Andalucían home is an oasis of tranquillity offering all modern comforts while retaining its historic charm. A full breakfast is included, and there are great views of the castle. No under-16s. ✆ C/Campito 35 • Map B3 • 959 12 77 78 • www.lacasanoble.net • Dis. access • €€€€€

4 La Casa Grande, Arcos de la Frontera

In 1729 the Nuñez de Prado family erected this mansion, which has preserved its original structure. Perched over the cliff of La Peña, terracotta floors, wood beams, stone columns, ceramic tiles, hand-woven bedspreads and antiques are among the many details. ✆ C/Maldonado 10 • Map C5 • 956 70 39 30 • www.lacasagrande.net • Closed 6 Jan–6 Feb • €€

5 Amanhavis Hotel, Benahavis

In the hills just outside Marbella, this place is like an Andalucían theme park, albeit very tasteful. Gardens and pools set off the nine rooms with names like "The Christopher Columbus Berth" and "The Spice Trader's Caravan" – all decorated accordingly. ✆ C/del Pilar 3 • Map D5 • 952 85 60 26/61 51 • www.amanhavis.com • Closed mid-Jan–mid-Feb • €€€

6 Hotel González, Córdoba

This charming hotel typifies the old houses of the Jewish Quarter, with a central patio and an elegant marble entrance replete with antiques and high ceilings. Many rooms look onto the patio. ✆ C/Manriquez 3 • Map D3 • 957 47 98 19 • www.hotel-gonzalez.com • €€

7 NH Amistad Córdoba

Five minutes' walk from La Mezquita and built into the old city walls. The large patio-cloisters are lovely, and there's also a plunge pool and sun terrace. ✆ Plaza de Maimónides 3 • Map D3 • 957 42 03 35 • www.nh-hotels.com • Dis. access • €€€

8 El Castillo, Castillo de Monda

If you're in the mood for Moorish opulence, this castle high above the town fits the bill. Elegant and rich furnishings, and a gourmet restaurant too. ✆ Avda de Castillo • Map D5 • 952 45 71 42 • www.castillodemonda.es • €€€

9 Hotel Palacete Santa Ana, Baeza

This hotel occupies a 16th-century palace, beautifully restored and set off with priceless antiques and paintings. ✆ C/Santa Ana Vieja 9 • Map F2 • 953 74 16 57 • www.palacetesantana.com • €€

10 Palacio de la Rambla, Úbeda

This 16th-century palace offers eight rooms for guests to experience the refined atmosphere. The patio is said to have been designed by Vandelvira himself. Breakfast included. ✆ Plaza del Marqués 1 • Map F2 • 953 75 01 96 • www.palaciodelarambla.com • €€€

Note that hotel prices can double during local festivals. For dates of festivals See pp60–61

Left **Hotel Francia y Paris** Right **Hotel Posada de Vallina**

🔟 Budget Charmers

1 Hotel Francia y Paris, Cádiz

The best choice in this old city. Situated on an inviting plaza, with a handsome exterior and a vast foyer, it's convenient to all the major sights. Comfortable rooms, some with balconies. ◈ *Plaza San Francisco 6 • Map B5 • 956 21 23 19 • www.hotelfrancia.com • €€€*

2 Doña Blanca, Jerez de la Frontera

For the price, this place is really rather grand, providing all the services you'd expect of more high-end properties and it's well located right in the centre of the city. The common areas and rooms are a little basic, but perfectly maintained, and the building has its own garage. ◈ *C/Bodegas 11 • Map B5 • 956 34 87 61 • www.hoteldonablanca. com • €€*

3 Hotel La Casa del Califa, Vejer de la Frontera

A sojourn at this hotel, created out of eight different houses including the 17th-century Casa del Juzgado, is like staying in a private house. Wonderful views, excellent service and a highly recommended restaurant. Buffet breakfast included. ◈ *Plaza de España 16 • Map C5 • 956 44 77 30 • www.lacasadel califa.com • €€*

4 Hotel Marqués de Torresoto, Arcos de la Frontera

This 17th-century mansion has been exquisitely converted into an extremely comfortable hotel. Sit in the porticoed inner courtyard or linger in the Baroque family chapel and soak up the age-old ambience. ◈ *C/Marqués de Torresoto 4 • Map C5 • 956 70 07 17 • www.hotel marquesdetorresoto.com • €€€*

5 Hotel Hacienda Posada de Vallina, Córdoba

Located in the heart of historic Córdoba, this house was built before the Mezquita, in AD 785, and combines the charm of a historic establishment with a range of modern amenities. Christopher Columbus stayed in what is now Room 204. ◈ *C/Corregidor Luis de la Cerda 83 • Map D3 • 957 49 87 50 • www. hhposadadevallina.es • €€€*

6 Hostal Miguel, Nerja

A family-run hostel in the heart of Nerja, convenient for the village's bars and restaurants. The accommodation is tastefully decorated with a Moroccan theme. Rooms are comfortable and have ceiling fans, fridges and are en-suite. There is a delightful roof terrace. ◈ *C/Almirante Ferrandiz 31 • Map E5 • 952 52 15 23 • www.hostalmiguel.com • €€*

7 Hostal Lineros, Córdoba

With its striking Mudéjar-style architecture, this building epitomizes the city's cross-cultural charm. It's a great choice in the old quarter. ◈ *C/Lineros 38 • Map D3 • hostallineros38.com • €€*

8 Hotel San Gabriel, Ronda

Built in 1736, this converted mansion, with its original coat of arms and handsome façade, offers remarkably sumptuous rooms for the price. ◈ *C/Marqués de Moctezuma 19 • Map D5 • 952 19 03 92 • www.hotel sangabriel.com • Closed 1–9 Jan, 19–31 Jul & 21–31 Dec • €€*

9 Cortijo Torrera, Castell del Ferro

Set in mountainous scenery but facing the sea (and with a pool too!), the structure maintains its rustic charm while providing many modern comforts. ◈ *Rambla de Lújar • Map F5 • 958 34 91 39 • www.torrera.com • No air-conditioning • €*

10 Hotel TRH, Baeza

Right in the heart of this Renaissance town is this oasis of quiet beauty. It's part of a chain, with all the conveniences, yet evokes timeless style. ◈ *C/Concepción 3 • Map F2 • 953 74 81 30 • www. trhhoteles.info • €€*

For budget hotels in Seville and Granada See pp138–9

Price Categories

For a standard, double room per night (with breakfast if included), taxes and extra charges.

€	under €50
€€	€50–€100
€€€	€100–€150
€€€€	€150–€200
€€€€€	over €200

Above **View from a terrace at Antonio**

🔟 Rural Retreats

1 Finca Buen Vino, Sierra de Aracena

Set amid green hills, this converted ranch is filled with an eclectic mix of furniture, paintings, pottery and books. Rooms are all distinctive, whether due to hand-painted walls, Oriental hangings, a bathtub with a view, or a fireplace. In spring, the valley below is filled with white heather, primroses and the sound of nightingales; summer days can be spent beside the pool. Self-catering cottages also available. ✪ Nr Los Marines, N433 km95 • Map A2 • 959 12 40 34 • www. fincabuenvino.com • €€€

2 Antonio, Zahara de los Atunes

This seaside retreat is decorated in a traditional style, with whitewashed walls, and there's a nice pool. Most rooms have terraces overlooking the sea. ✪ Atlanterra km1 • Map C6 • 956 43 91 41 • www.antoniohoteles.com • Dis. access • €€€

3 Alcázar de la Reina, Carmona

In the historic centre of this small town the façade of this hotel stands out, while the interior reflects the style of Mudéjar craftsmanship. No two rooms are alike, but they all have marble bathrooms, and several enjoy spectacular views. ✪ Plaza de Lasso 2 • Map C3 • 954 19 62 00 • www.alcazar-reina.es • €€€

4 Hotel Humaina, Montes de Málaga

This is a small, family-run hotel, set in the mountains, and the emphasis is on relaxation, whether that is reading a book in the library, swimming in the pool or enjoying a glass of Málaga wine. Cycling, horse riding and rambling are also on offer. ✪ Ctra Colmenar • Map E5 • 952 64 10 25 • www.hotelhumaina.es • €€

5 Alquería de los Lentos, Niguelas

At the foothills of the Sierra Nevada surrounded by orchards, this 16th-century mill has been lovingly transformed into a small hotel and organic restaurant. The property boasts a hamman, and most rooms have fireplaces and terraces. ✪ Camino de los Molinos s/n • Map F4 • 958 77 78 50 • www.alquerialoslentos.com • €€

6 La Posada del Ángel, Ojén

Situated just 15 minutes from Marbella in the white-washed town of Ojén in the Sierra de las Nieves, this posada has just 17 rooms. Special painting holidays can be organised which include tours of the local area, and the owners can also organise other activities. ✪ C/Mesones 21 • Map D5 • 952 88 18 08 • www.laposadadelangel.com • €€

7 Cuevas La Granja, near Benalúa

A complex of restored cave dwellings, each of which preserves their original style. The location provides the perfect setting for rest and relaxation. ✪ Camino de la Granja • Map F3 • 958 67 60 00 • www.cuevas.org • No air-conditioning • €€

8 Cuevas Pedro Antonio de Alarcón, Guadix

A charming cave dwelling with modern comforts. Beautiful views over the city of Guadix and the Sierra Nevada. There's a pool too. ✪ Bda San Torcuato • Map F4 • 958 66 49 86 • www.cuevaspedro antonio.es • Dis. access • No air-conditioning • €€

9 Finca Listonero, Turre

This converted farmhouse is owned and run by two Australian restaurateurs. Generous homemade breakfasts and made-to-order dinners. ✪ Cortijo Grande • Map H4 • 950 47 90 94 • www. fincalistonero.com • €€

10 Cortijo El Sotillo, San José

A tranquil base from which to explore the beaches of Cabo de Gata. Rooms are spacious, with large terraces. ✪ Ctra Entrada a San José • Map H5 • 950 61 11 00 • www. cortijoelsotillo.com • Dis. access • €€€

Note: Unless otherwise stated, all hotels accept credit cards, have en-suite bathrooms and air-conditioning

Left & Right **Cantueso, Periana**

TOP 10 Self-Catering Options

1 Casas Rurales Los Gallos, Almonaster la Real

Whitewashed cottages are set amid woods, patios, arcades, pools and flowers. Each one has a different feel and colour scheme, and all are loaded with rustic charm and antiques as well as modern conveniences. ✪ *Finca Los Gallos, Estación de Almonaster • Map B3 • 687 36 57 54 • www.alojamientolosgallos.com • Dis. access • No credit cards • No air-conditioning • €€*

2 Villa Turística Grazalema

Despite the price, this is a fairly luxurious choice for those who want their own apartment. The property includes a hotel, the homes, a pool, parking and a bar-café. The terrace, offering views of the mountains, is surrounded by gardens. ✪ *Ctra Olivar • Map C5 • 956 13 21 36 • www.tugasa.com • No air-conditioning • €€*

3 Casas Karen, Costa de la Luz

Typical Andalucían houses and apartments, and native-style straw roof bungalows, nestle between pinewoods and the beach. Follow signs to Faro de Trafalgar. ✪ *Fuente del Madroño 6, nr Cabo Trafalgar • Map C6 • 956 43 70 67 • www.casaskaren.com • No air-conditioning • €€€*

4 Apartamentos Murillo, Seville

These lovely apartments are named after the Baroque painter who hailed from the Barrio de Santa Cruz, right in the middle of this flower-decked old quarter. The group that owns the apartments also runs a hotel (C/Lope de Rueda 9). ✪ *C/Reinosa 6 • Map M4 • 954 21 60 95 • www.hotelmurillo.com • €€*

5 El Molino de la Quinta, Constantina

This rustic Andalucian farmhouse has seven apartments, each housing between four and six people. The modern and comfortable accommo-dation is set in lovely grounds. ✪ *C/Pozuelo, "Finca la Quinta" • Map C3 • 678 45 64 02 • www.elmolinodelaquinta.com • No air-conditioning • €€*

6 Hostal La Posada, Mijas

A great opportunity to rent a fully equipped apartment in this attractive town and to sample a bit of the real Andalucía. ✪ *C/Coin 47 & 49 • Map D5 • 952 48 53 10 • No credit cards • No air-conditioning • €*

7 Hacienda La Colorá, Montoro

You can go for a studio, an apartment or a grand suite in this 18th-century country mansion. It's a garden of loveliness, cultivating olives and honey, and there's a beautiful pool. If you like, you can take painting classes. ✪ *9 km (6 miles) NW of Montoro along the CO414 • Map E2 • 957 33 60 77 • www.lacolora.com • No air-conditioning • €€€*

8 Casas Rurales Benarum, Mecina Bombarón

The 12 rural cabins each house between two and five people and are nestled in this quiet mountain town. The stylish cabins are fully equipped and there is a pool and spa in the grounds. ✪ *C/ Casas Blancas 1 • Map F4 • 958 851 149 • www.benarum.com • €€*

9 Cantueso, Periana

This complex offers ten white-washed cottages with private terraces in a splendid mountainside setting. Lush gardens provide tranquillity. ✪ *Periana, Málaga • Map E4 • 699 94 62 13 • www.cantueso.net • Some dis. access • Some air-conditioning • €€*

10 Santa Ana Apartamentos Turísticos, Granada

Situated just above the river, these apartments come with views of the Albaicín quarter. Each apartment has large, comfortable rooms with stylish decor. Minimum two nights stay. ✪ *Puente Cabrera 9 • Map F4 • 958 22 81 30 • www.apartamentos-santaana.com • €€*

→ *For quality, well-maintained apartments in Seville or Granada, visit www.friendlyrentals.com*

Above **Hostal Séneca**

Price Categories

For a double room per night, including taxes and extra charges, a night's camping fee or a night in self-catering.

€ under €50
€€ €50–€100
€€€ €100–€150
€€€€ €150–€200
€€€€€ over €200

🔟 Hostals and Camping

1 Hostal La Malagueña, Estepona

Although it isn't an official hostel or even aimed at backpackers, the price doesn't get any better than this. The airy rooms have balconies facing the square. You can stroll along the sandy beaches or wander around the shops of this old and still authentic fishing village. ◉ *C/Castillo 1 • Map D5 • 952 80 00 11 • www.hlm estepona.com • No air-conditioning • €*

2 Hotel San Francisco, Ronda

This budget hotel has pleasant, clean rooms with basic amenities such as TV and air-conditioning, as well as large bathrooms. Some rooms have balconies with mountain views. ◉ *C/María Cabrera 18 • Map D5 • 952 87 32 99 • hotelronda@terra.es • Dis. access • €*

3 Hostel, Marbella

Double rooms, some with adjoining bath, a pool, and lots of recreational options make this an excellent youth hostel. It's just north of the lovely old quarter, where you can see the real Marbella and not just the glitz. Walk through it to get to the beach and the port. ◉ *C/Trapiche 2 • Map D5 • 951 27 03 01 • www. inturjoven.com • Dis. access • No credit cards • No air-conditioning • €*

4 Hostal Séneca, Córdoba

Friendly and delightful, as well as excellent value. Stained-glass windows on the first floor and a patio with Moorish touches add to the grace. Some rooms have en-suite bathrooms. Book ahead. ◉ *C/Conde y Luque • Map D3 • 957 47 32 34 • No credit cards • No air-conditioning • €*

5 Hostel, Málaga

Modern double rooms and a sun-terrace make this an acceptable option. Although not particularly near to the centre, it's well connected by public transport. ◉ *Plaza Pio XII 6 • Map E5 • 951 30 81 70 • www.inturjoven.com • Dis. access • No credit cards • No en-suite bathrooms • No air-conditioning • €*

6 Instalación Juvenil, Solynieve, Sierra Nevada

Located near the top of the ski station, with rooms holding two to six, ideal for skiers in the winter or trekkers in the summer. They will also rent skis and other equipment. ◉ *C/Peñones 22 • Map F4 • 958 57 51 16 • www.inturjoven.com • Dis. access • No air-conditioning • €*

7 Instalación Campamento Chipiona

A couple of kilometres from the beach, this campsite has rental tents, swimming pool, TV room, dining area and sports facilities. ◉ *Pinar de la Villa • Map B5 • 956 37 12 92 • No credit cards • No air-conditioning • €*

8 Camping El Sur, Ronda

Camping and bungalows are available here. It's a chance to take beautiful walks or horse-ride in the countryside around Ronda. ◉ *Ctra Ronda-Algeciras km1.5 • Map D5 • 952 87 59 39 • www.campingelsur.com • Dis. access • No credit cards • No en-suite facilities • No air-conditioning • €–€€*

9 Camping Cabo de Gata, Cabo de Gata

This campsite offers shady areas for tents, trailers and RV hook-ups, as well as bungalows. Facilities include a pool, access to pristine beaches and a reception centre with safes. ◉ *Ctra Cabo de Gata, Cortijo Ferrón • Map H5 • 950 16 04 43 • www.campingcabodegata. com • Dis. access • No credit cards • €*

10 Camping Sierra Nevada, Granada

One of the most convenient camping choices in the region, with big, clean bathrooms, a pool and a laundry. There is also a budget motel. ◉ *Avda de Madrid 107 • Map F4 • 958 15 00 62 • www. campingsierranevada.com • Closed Nov–Feb • Dis. access • No credit cards • €–€€*

General Index

Acknowledgements

Main Contributor
American-born Jeffrey Kennedy now lives mainly in Italy and Spain. A graduate of Stanford University, he divides his time between producing, acting and writing.
He is the co-author of *Top 10 Rome* and the author of the Top 10 guides to *Mallorca, Miami and the Keys* and *San Francisco*.

Produced by Sargasso Media Ltd, London

Editorial Director Zoë Ross
Art Editor Janis Utton
Picture Research Monica Allende
Proofreader Stewart J Wild
Indexer Hilary Bird
Editorial Assistance Cristina Barrallo

Main Photographer
Peter Wilson
Additional Photographers
Neil Lukas, John Miller, Linda Whitwam
Illustrator
chrisorr.com

FOR DORLING KINDERSLEY
Publisher Douglas Amrine
Publishing Manager Anna Streiffert
Managing Art Editor Jane Ewart
Senior Cartographic Editor Casper Morris
DTP Jason Little
Production Melanie Dowland
Maps James Macdonald, Mapping Ideas Ltd

Additional Contributors
Francisco Bastida, Michel Cruz, Conrad van Dyk, Claire Jones, Nicola Malone, Lynnette McCurdy, Caroline Mead, Pete Quinlan, Mani Ramaswamy, Sands Publishing Solutions, Karen Villabona, Word on Spain.

Picture Credits
t-top; tc-top centre; tr-top right; cla-centre left above; ca-centre above; cra-centre right above; cl-centre left; c-centre; cr-centre right; clb-centre left below; cb-centre below; crb-centre right below; bl-below left; bc-below centre; br-below right.
Every effort has been made to trace the copyright holders, and we apologize in advance for any unintentional omissions. We would be pleased to insert the appropriate acknowledgements in any subsequent edition of this publication.

The publishers would like to thank the following individuals, companies, and picture libraries for permission to reproduce their photographs:

ABADES GROUP: 85tl; AISA, Barcelona: 7b, 13t, 23cr, 29t, 30b, 30–31, 31cra, 31crb, 31b, 32–3, 34t, 35r, 44tr, 44tl, 50b, 50tr, 52tr, 56tl, 56tr, 56b, 57b, 57r, 58tl, 60b, 61r, 66tr, 66b, 67cl, 87t, 87b, 90 tr, 97t. 134tc; ALAMY IMAGES: Felipe Rodriguez 15cl; Ken Welsh 18crb; ANTONIO HOTELES: 145tl; CORBIS: 103tl, 103tr; COVER, Madrid: 13b, 34b. www.dreamers-disco.com, Marbella: 104tl. GETTY IMAGES: 1. HOTEL CASTILLO DE MONDA: 143tl; HOTEL PARAISO DEL MAR: 142tl. LEONARDO MEDIABANK: 141t. PENA EL TARANTO: photo Enrique Capilla, Paco Cortés y El Polaco Premio Guitarra performing115tl; MARCO POLO, Madrid : 30t, 31t, 33crb. JOSE LUCAS RUIZ: 17clb. SALA MALANDAR: 84tl. TORRE DE LA CALAHORRA: 19bc; TOURIST OFFICE, Andalucia: 59c, 59r, 60tl, 60tr, 61t, 62tr, 93t, 135tr

All other images are © Dorling Kindersley. For further information see: www.dkimages.com

Phrase Book

In an Emergency

Help!	**¡Socorro!**	soh-koh-roh
Stop!	**¡Pare!**	pah-reh
Call a doctor!	**¡Llame a un médico!**	yah-meh ah oon meh-dee-koh
Call an ambulance!	**¡Llame a una ambulancia!**	yah-meh ah oonah ahm-boo-lahn-thee-ah
Call the police!	**¡Llame a la policía!**	yah-meh ah lah poh-lee-thee-ah
Call the fire brigade!	**¡Llame a los bomberos!**	yah-meh ah lohs bohm-beh-rohs
Where is the nearest telephone?	**¿Dónde está el teléfono más próximo?**	dohn-deh ehs-tah teh-leh-foh-noh mahs prohx-ee-moh
Where is the nearest hospital?	**¿Dónde está el hospital más próximo?**	dohn-deh ehs-tah ehl ohs-pee-tahl mahs prohx-ee-moh

Communication Essentials

Yes	**Sí**	see
No	**No**	noh
Please	**Por favor**	pohr fah-vohr
Thank you	**Gracias**	grah-thee-ahs
Excuse me	**Perdone**	pehr-doh-neh
Hello	**Hola**	oh-lah
Goodbye	**Adiós**	ah-dee-ohs
Good night	**Buenas noches**	bweh-nahs noh-chehs
Morning	**La mañana**	lah mah-nyah-nah
Afternoon	**La tarde**	lah tahr-deh
Evening	**La tarde**	lah tahr-deh
Yesterday	**Ayer**	ah-yehr
Today	**Hoy**	oy
Tomorrow	**Mañana**	mah-nya-nah
Here	**Aquí**	ah-kee
There	**Allí**	ah-yee
What?	**¿Qué?**	keh
When?	**¿Cuándo?**	kwahn-doh
Why?	**¿Por qué?**	pohr-keh
Where?	**¿Dónde?**	dohn-deh

Useful Phrases

How are you?	**¿Cómo está usted?**	koh-moh ehs-tah oos-tehd
Very well, thank you	**Muy bien, gracias**	mwee bee-ehn grah-thee-ahs
Pleased to meet you.	**Encantado de conocerle.**	ehn-kahn-tah-doh deh koh-noh-thehr-leh
See you soon	**Hasta pronto**	ahs-tah proh-toh
That's fine	**Está bien**	ehs-tah bee-ehn
Where is/are ...?	**¿Dónde está/están ...?**	dohn-deh ehs-tah/ehs-tahn
How far is it to ...?	**¿Cuántos metros/ kilómetros hay de aquí a ...?**	kwahn-tohs meh-trohs/kee-loh-meh-trohs eye deh ah-kee ah
Which way to ...?	**¿Por dónde se va a ...?**	pohr dohn-deh seh bah ah
Do you speak English?	**¿Habla inglés?**	ah-blah een-glehs
I don't understand	**No comprendo**	noh kohm-prehn-doh
Could you speak more slowly please?	**¿Puede hablar más despacio por favor?**	pweh-deh ah-blahr mahs dehs-pah-thee-oh pohr fah-vohr
I'm sorry	**Lo siento**	loh see-ehn-toh

Useful Words

big	**grande**	grahn-deh
small	**pequeño**	peh-keh-nyoh
hot	**caliente**	kah-lee-ehn-teh
cold	**frío**	free-oh
good	**bueno**	bweh-noh
bad	**malo**	mah-loh
enough	**bastante**	bahs-tahn-teh
well	**bien**	bee-ehn
open	**abierto**	ah-bee-ehr-toh
closed	**cerrado**	thehr-rah-doh
left	**izquierda**	eeth-key-ehr-dah
right	**derecha**	deh-reh-chah
straight on	**todo recto**	toh-doh rehk-toh
near	**cerca**	thehr-kah
far	**lejos**	leh-hohs
up	**arriba**	ah-ree-bah
down	**abajo**	ah-bah-hoh
early	**temprano**	tehm-prah-noh
late	**tarde**	tahr-deh
entrance	**entrada**	ehn-trah-dah
exit	**salida**	sah-lee-dah
toilet	**lavabos, servicios**	lah-vah-bohs, sehr-bee-thee-ohs
more	**más**	mahs
less	**menos**	meh-nohs

Shopping

How much does this cost?	**¿Cuánto cuesta ésto?**	kwahn-toh kwehs-tah ehs-toh
I would like ...	**Me gustaría ...**	meh goos-ta-ree-ah
Do you have?	**¿Tienen?**	tee-yeh-nehn
I'm just looking	**Sólo estoy mirando**	soh-loh ehs-toy mee-rahn-doh
Do you take credit cards?	**¿Aceptan tarjetas de crédito?**	ah-thehp-tahn deh kreh-dee-toh
What time do you open?	**¿A qué hora abren?**	ah keh oh-rah ah-brehn
What time do you close?	**¿A qué hora cierran?**	ah keh oh-rah thee-ehr-rahn
This one	**Éste**	ehs-teh
That one	**Ése**	eh-seh
expensive	**caro**	kahr-oh
cheap	**barato**	bah-rah-toh
size, clothes	**talla**	tah-yah
size, shoes	**número**	noo-mehr-oh
white	**blanco**	blahn-koh
black	**negro**	neh-groh
red	**rojo**	roh-hoh
yellow	**amarillo**	ah-mah-ree-yoh
green	**verde**	behr-deh
blue	**azul**	ah-thool
antiques shop	**la tienda de antigüedades**	lah tee-ehn-dah deh ahn-tee-gweh-dah-dehs
bakery	**la panadería**	lah pah-nah-deh-ree-ah
bank	**el banco**	ehl bahn-koh
bookshop	**la librería**	lah lee-breh-ree-ah
butcher's	**la carnicería**	lah kahr-nee-theh-ree-ah
cake shop	**la pastelería**	lah pahs-teh-leh-ree-ah
chemist's	**la farmacia**	lah fahr-mah-thee-ah
fishmonger's	**la pescadería**	lah pehs-kah-deh-ree-ah
greengrocer's	**la frutería**	lah froo-teh-ree-ah
grocer's	**la tienda de comestibles**	lah tee-yehn-dah deh koh-mehs-tee-blehs
hairdresser's	**la peluquería**	lah peh-loo-keh-ree-ah
market	**el mercado**	ehl mehr-kah-doh
newsagent's	**el kiosko de prensa**	ehl kee-ohs-koh deh prehn-sah
post office	**la oficina de correos**	lah oh-fee-thee-nah deh kohr-reh-ohs
shoe shop	**la zapatería**	lah thah-pah-teh-ree-ah
supermarket	**el supermercado**	ehl soo-pehr-mehr-kah-doh
tobacconist	**el estanco**	ehl ehs-tahn-koh
travel agency	**la agencia de viajes**	lah ah-hehn-thee-ah deh bee-ah-hehs

Sightseeing

art gallery	**el museo de arte**	ehl moo-seh-oh deh ahr-teh
cathedral	**la catedral**	lah kah-teh-drahl
church	**la iglesia**	lah ee-gleh-see-ah
	la basílica	lah bah-see-lee-kah
garden	**el jardín**	ehl hahr-deen
library	**la biblioteca**	lah bee-blee-oh-teh-kah
museum	**el museo**	ehl moo-seh-oh
tourist information office	**la oficina de turismo**	lah oh-fee-thee nah deh too-rees-moh
town hall	**el ayuntamiento**	ehl ah-yoon-tah-mee-ehn-toh
closed for holiday	**cerrado por vacaciones**	thehr-rah-doh pohr bah-kah-thee-oh-nehs
bus station	**la estación de autobuses**	lah ehs-tah-thee-ohn deh owtoh-buo-sehs
railway station	**la estación de trenes**	lah ehs-tah-thee-ohn deh treh-nehs

Staying in a Hotel

Do you have a vacant room?	¿Tiene una habitación libre?	tee-eh-neh oo-nah ah-bee-tah-thee-ohn lee-breh
double room	habitación doble	ah-bee-tah-thee-ohn doh-bleh
with double bed	con cama de matrimonio	kohn kah-mah deh mah-tree-moh-nee-oh
twin room	habitación con dos camas	ah-bee-tah-thee-ohn kohn dohs kah-mahs
single room	habitación individual	ah-bee-tah-thee-ohn een-dee-vee-doo-ahl
room with a bath	habitación con baño	ah-bee-tah-thee-ohn kohn bah-nyoh
shower	ducha	doo-chah
porter	el botones	ehl boh-toh-nehs
key	la llave	lah yah-veh
I have a reservation	Tengo una habitación reservada	tehn-goh oo-na ah-bee-tah-thee-ohn reh-sehr-bah-dah

Eating Out

Have you got a table for . . .?	¿Tiene mesa para . . .?	tee-eh-neh meh-sah pah-rah
I want to reserve a table	Quiero reservar una mesa	kee-eh-roh reh-sehr-bahr oo-nah meh-sah
The bill	La cuenta	lah kwehn-tah
I am a vegetarian	Soy vegetariano/a	soy beh-heh-tah-ree-ah-no/na
waitress/ waiter	camarera/ camarero	kah-mah-reh-rah/ kah-mah-reh-roh
menu	la carta	lah kahr-tah
fixed-price menu	menú del día	meh-noo dehl dee-ah
wine list	la carta de vinos	lah kahr-tah deh bee-nohs
glass	un vaso	oon bah-soh
bottle	una botella	oo-nah boh-teh-yah
knife	un cuchillo	oon koo-chee-yoh
fork	un tenedor	oon teh-neh-dohr
spoon	una cuchara	oo-nah koo-chah-rah
breakfast	el desayuno	ehl deh-sah-yoo-noh
lunch	la comida/ el almuerzo	lah koh-mee-dah/ ehl ahl-mwehr-thoh
dinner	la cena	lah theh-nah
main course	el primer plato	ehl pree-mehr plah-toh
starters	los entremeses	lohs ehn-treh-meh-ses
dish of the day	el plato del día	ehl plah-toh dehl dee-ah
coffee	el café	ehl kah-feh
rare (meat)	poco hecho	poh-koh eh-choh
medium	medio hecho	meh-dee-oh eh-choh
well done	muy hecho	mwee eh-choh

Menu Decoder

al horno	ahl ohr-noh	baked
asado	ah-sah-doh	roast
el aceite	ah-thee-eh-teh	oil
las aceitunas	ah-theh-toon-ahs	olives
el agua mineral	ah-gwa mee-neh-rahl	mineral water
sin gas/con gas	seen gas/kohn gas	still/sparkling
el ajo	ah-hoh	garlic
el arroz	ahr-rohth	rice
el azúcar	ah-thoo-kahr	sugar
la carne	kahr-neh	meat
la cebolla	theh-boh-yah	onion
el cerdo	therh-doh	pork
la cerveza	thehr-beh-thah	beer
el chocolate	choh-koh-lah-teh	chocolate
el chorizo	choh-ree-thoh	spicy sausage
el cordero	kohr-deh-roh	lamb
el fiambre	fee-ahm-breh	cold meat
frito	free-toh	fried
la fruta	froo-tah	fruit
los frutos secos	froo-tohs seh-kohs	nuts
las gambas	gahm-bahs	prawns
el helado	eh-lah-doh	ice cream
el huevo	oo-eh-voh	egg
el jamón serrano	hah-mohn sehr-rah-noh	cured ham
el jerez	heh-rehz	sherry
la langosta	lahn-gohs-tah	lobster
la leche	leh-cheh	milk
el limón	lee-mohn	lemon
la limonada	lee-moh-nah-dah	lemonade
la mantequilla	mahn-teh-kee-yah	butter

la manzana	mahn-thah-nah	apple
los mariscos	mah-rees-kohs	seafood
la menestra	meh-nehs-trah	vegetable stew
la naranja	nah-rahn-hah	orange
el pan	pahn	bread
el pastel	pahs-tehl	cake
las patatas	pah-tah-tahs	potatoes
el pescado	pehs-kah-doh	fish
la pimienta	pee-mee-yehn-tah	pepper
el plátano	plah-tah-noh	banana
el pollo	poh-yoh	chicken
el postre	pohs-treh	dessert
el queso	keh-soh	cheese
la sal	sahl	salt
la salsa	sahl-sah	sauce
seco	seh-koh	dry
el solomillo	soh-loh-mee-yoh	sirloin
la sopa	soh-pah	soup
la tarta	tahr-tah	pie/cake
el té	teh	tea
la ternera	tehr-neh-rah	beef
el vinagre	bee-nah-greh	vinegar
el vino blanco	bee-noh blahn-koh	white wine
el vino rosado	bee-noh roh-sah-doh	rosé wine
el vino tinto	bee-noh teen-toh	red wine

Numbers

0	cero	theh-roh
1	uno	oo-noh
2	dos	dohs
3	tres	trehs
4	cuatro	kwa-troh
5	cinco	theen-koh
6	seis	says
7	siete	see-eh-teh
8	ocho	oh-choh
9	nueve	nweh-veh
10	diez	dee-ehth
11	once	ohn-theh
12	doce	doh-theh
13	trece	treh-theh
14	catorce	kah-tohr-theh
15	quince	keen-theh
16	dieciséis	dee-eh-thee-seh-ees
17	diecisiete	dee-eh-thee-see-eh-teh
18	dieciocho	dee-eh-thee-oh-choh
19	diecinueve	dee-eh-thee-nweh-veh
20	veinte	beh-een-teh
21	veintiuno	beh-een-tee-oo-noh
22	veintidós	beh-een-tee-dohs
30	treinta	treh-een-tah
31	treinta y uno	treh-een-tah yee oo-noh
40	cuarenta	kwah-rehn-tah
50	cincuenta	theen-kwehn-tah
60	sesenta	seh-sehn-tah
70	setenta	seh-tehn-tah
80	ochenta	oh-chehn-tah
90	noventa	noh-vehn-tah
100	cien	thee-ehn
101	ciento uno	thee-ehn-toh oo-noh
200	doscientos	dohs-thee-ehn-tohs
500	quinientos	khee-nee-ehn-tohs
700	setecientos	seh-teh-thee-ehn-tohs
900	novecientos	noh-veh-thee-ehn-tohs
1,000	mil	meel
1,001	mil uno	meel oo-noh

Time

one minute	un minuto	oon mee-noo-toh
one hour	una hora	oo-na oh-rah
half an hour	media hora	meh-dee-a oh-rah
Monday	lunes	loo-nehs
Tuesday	martes	mahr-tehs
Wednesday	miércoles	mee-ehr-koh-lehs
Thursday	jueves	hoo-weh-vehs
Friday	viernes	bee-ehr-nehs
Saturday	sábado	sah-bah-doh
Sunday	domingo	doh-meen-goh